HANGING ON

THE GREAT DEPRESSION
THROUGH A CHILD'S EYES

CYNTHIA RESTIVO
ILLUSTRATED BY LINDA KNOLL

Published in the United States by the Word Project Press of Sonora, CA

Requests for permission to make copies of any part of this work should be submitted online at info@wordprojectpress.com

Cover Design: Melody Baker

ISBN-13: 978-0-989068277
ISBN-10: 0989068277

HANGING ON

is dedicated to
George Hibbard Moore
April 5, 1923 – April 15, 2010

George Hibbard "Brubby" Moore can be found in every story in this collection, and if he were alive today his versions of them would have added richly to the telling. He was a loving, patient brother, and throughout their childhood, Marian was his faithful shadow.

During World War II, he served in the Pacific Theater as a First Lieutenant pilot in the Army Air Corps. After the war, Hibbard settled in Morro Bay and worked as a photographer and photo technician. As a photo tech at Aerospace Corp., he worked on the Gemini program and the Apollo space missions. Hibbard was on a team responsible for developing film brought back from the Apollo missions including the photos taken on July 16, 1969, as man first walked on the moon. Moving to Oregon, he bought a 350-acre farm where he raised livestock and also worked at the local lumber mill. He grew up working and never quit. He believed in working until he couldn't work anymore, never wasting time or money.

Hibbard died at age 87 and was survived by his three children, Pamela Rodriguez, Gary Moore, and John Moore, and was preceded in death by his wife of 51 years, Barbara Moore. Hibbard enjoyed life: he loved attending air shows and races, fishing for steelhead and salmon, was an avid rock hound, and according to the family, had quite a "gift of gab." Oh, the stories he could tell....

Contents

Depression* and that I was developing a storytelling program based on oral histories* of the 1930s called "Brother, Can You Spare a Dime?" I became fascinated with Marian's story. At that time, I did not even consider writing a book, but here we are eight years later and you are reading what has evolved.

Marian and I met periodically: sometimes a couple of meetings in a week, while other times, months passed between our visits. Often during our interviews or listening to them afterwards, I thought of my own grandparents, great aunts and uncles, and my husband's parents, all of whom weathered the Depression with resourcefulness and resilience. Interviewing Marian gave me a glimpse into the human spirit and strength that are called into action during hard times.

With each interview, we probed deeper, searching for greater clarity, until I began to sense the texture of Marian's life, the feel of her environment, the sound of the other characters in her story, the color of the objects that surrounded her each day. Piecing together this book became like putting together a jigsaw puzzle with some of the pieces missing.

Marian had a brother who was the other living witness to her stories. He had a reputation for being a fabulous storyteller and had vivid memories of his childhood. Before calling him, I wanted to be sure I was asking the best questions to get what I needed to fill in where Marian's memory faltered. He lived several hours away and with my busy schedule finding a time for an in-person interview was problematic. I would need special equipment to record the interview over the phone. Finally, I located and learned to use the fancy recording equipment. Confident that Hibbard would be able to fill in details and perhaps clarify factual uncertainties, I contacted him in April 2010, the same week he went into the hospital, just days before he died. He was too weak to talk with me.

There is an old Italian saying, "When an old man dies, an entire library closes."

And that, dear readers, is probably the most difficult lesson learned during this project. If you have an elder you have been meaning to interview, don't wait. Even if the questions are not perfect, even if your equipment is not perfect, just do it! Today, this week, this month. When it comes to interviewing elders, the perfect question is the one asked and the perfect equipment is the one used — even if it is just your ears. Then if time is kind, you can go back and re-interview or ask follow-up questions after the initial interview.

The best hours I spent were those sitting across from Marian at her dining room table listening to her life experiences. You never know a person's story until you stop to listen.

An appendix is included at the end of this book — organized by each story — that will give you additional information about the historical times when Marian grew up, some of her Mother's and Grandmother's recipes, and interesting facts that didn't quite fit into the book. An entry in the appendix will be indicated by an asterisk (*) in the stories. If you are interested in collecting your family stories, you will find tips on how to do that in the appendix, as well.

I hope this book inspires you to stop and listen to a story lived by someone you care about. If you would like help getting started or you have any questions about this book, oral history, or storytelling, you can contact me through my website: www.cynthiarestivo.com

Stories remind us we are not alone on this journey.

- Cynthia Restivo
November 2014

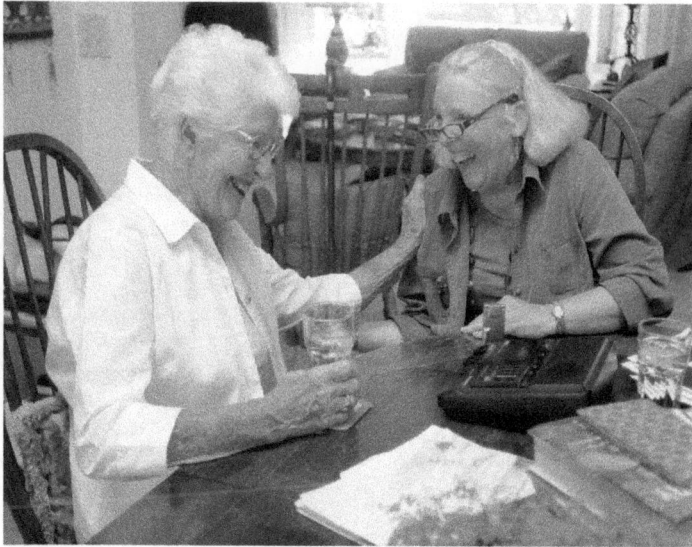

Photo Courtesy of Union Democrat

Marian and Cynthia during an interview.

A Note from Marian

This is a time of reflection, an attempt to bring back a bit of history, a time in California when a little girl and her family lived, worked, and played through the Great Depression. I hope to elicit an understanding of those years from a child's point of view.

I was born in 1925 in Torrance, California, but my story actually begins a few years later in an orange grove in a small Southern California town and travels through mining communities of the Sierra Nevada Mountains to an orchard in the Central Valley and settles finally in San Jose. During these years, we lived in a couple rooms my father built onto the end of a long chicken house, a tent, a one-room cabin, a three-bedroom house with a lawn, and a big house in San Jose where we took in boarders to help pay the rent. In each of these places, my brother, Hibbard, and I reveled in many adventures together.

Looking back at my childhood has brought me in touch with who and what shaped me into the woman I am. I truly believe God had a plan to help me see life as a gift. Hibbard and I didn't understand how poor we were. Having very little,

7

we made do with what we had, or we did without. Our imagination made our experiences rich. The country was going through the Great Depression, but for my brother and me these were happy years.

– Marian Wolfe
November 2014

California Map

- Willows

Placerville
Sacramento
Sutter Creek • West Point
Glencoe
• Stockton

• San Jose

• Fort Ord

• Tulare

Hoover Dam
•

• Mohave

San Gabriel Dam
•
• Fontana
Santa Monica

Marian's California

It Began with a Crash

Mother worried about Grandma and Grandpa as Daddy read the newspaper out loud each night, "They say this is 'the worst crash in history,' that October 29, 1929, will be known as 'Black Tuesday.' The banks closed."

"How can they close the banks?" asked Mother.

"The reporter says, 'the bankers closed their doors and locked themselves in.' Apparently, they were afraid. They sneaked out the back door in the middle of the night," answered Daddy.

"When does it say the banks will open again?"

"No one knows. They think some might not ever open again," said Daddy. "All across the nation fortunes are lost."

Marian's parents had no money in banks and no fortune to lose, but her grandparents did. Having no phone, Mother had to wait until Sunday to find out how the crash affected them.

Finally, it was Sunday afternoon. Each week Grandma, Grandpa, and their friends, Mr. and Mrs. Quass, came out from Santa Monica to Fontana for dinner. Mother and the children dug up the potatoes for potato salad. They took out vegetables preserved in jars at the end of summer. Mother baked a fruit pie and, of course, fried chicken. Everything they ate was grown on their farm or traded for something grown on their farm.

Marian's grandparents had a beautiful house with a big dining room right on the beach in Santa Monica. But each week they drove 70 miles and squeezed around Marian's family table because the farm animals needed to be cared for: the goat, rabbits, dogs, cats and chickens. Fontana Farms,* a real estate company, had sold her father a ten-acre orange grove and the idea that the chickens would give them an income until the oranges were mature enough to provide for the family. After Daddy built the chicken coop to house 2000 chickens, he added two more rooms at the end for the family to live in until they had enough money to build a real house. One room was the kitchen, living room, and dining room while the other was where the family slept. The bathroom was an outhouse, a little shed outside with a hole in the ground.

Mother set the table with eight plates hoping they would all come. Marian helped Mother, climbing up on a pillow that lay on her chair to put a napkin under each fork.

When they got home from church, Daddy had already killed and plucked the chickens. Daddy did it when Marian was busy doing something else.

"Marian's too young to see the animals die," Daddy told Hibbard. "She's only four years old. She might have nightmares."

Being two years older, Hibbard was expected to help, protect and care for Marian.

But a couple of weeks earlier, Marian had seen. Marian and Hibbard were playing hide and go seek in the orange grove. While she hid near the coop behind an orange tree, she heard a chicken squawking. She peeked out from behind the tree to see Daddy taking a chicken to the stump in back of the chicken coop and chopping off its head. Marian completely forgot she was supposed to be hiding; the chicken was running around with no head. Hibbard tagged her.

"Marian that's not a very good hiding place. You're it! "

"Brubby, Look!"

"What?"

"The chicken."

"Oh, Marian, you're too young to see that." Hibbard put his hands over Marian's eyes and turned her around. She pulled his hand down and looked back at the chicken.

"But, Brubby, it doesn't have a head! How can a chicken run without a head?"

"I don't know, Sis. It's what chickens do before they die."

"I guess they don't want to die."

"I guess not."

"Maybe they think they won't die if they keep trying to live."

So Marian had seen, but she kept it a secret.

Before church this Sunday, Mother made potato salad and got the green beans ready to heat up. She would start frying up the chicken when she returned home. Mother's lemon meringue pie,* baked yesterday, sat on the counter waiting for everyone to get there, for everyone to eat, for the conversation to ping pong around the table, for the coffee to be poured, and only then would Marian be able to devour her slice of pie. Midday, car tires crunched on the long gravel driveway. Marian and Hibbard ran out.

Mr. and Mrs. Quass were opposites of Grandpa and Grandma. Mr. and Mrs. Quass were round and short while Grandpa and Grandma were tall and thin. Mr. and Mrs. Quass sounded like a gaggle of geese always talking over each other.

Grandpa and Grandma were quiet, only talking when they had something to say. But Mr. and Mrs. Quass laughed easily, and so it was always fun when they came.

When Grandpa turned off the engine to his Willys-Knight car, Marian heard Mrs. Quass talking. Marian ran up to Grandma, gave her a hug, and breathed in her rose perfume.

"Did you find your money?"

"What, Honey?"

"Mother said that you might not come because you lost your money."

All the adults gave each other silent looks, and then Grandma said, "I wouldn't miss a Sunday dinner with you, Dolly."

"Aren't you a dear," said Mrs. Quass pulling Marian to her. As Mrs. Quass squeezed, the four-year-old disappeared beneath folds of well-fed flesh. Marian lifted her chin and gasped for air as Mrs. Quass' body closed around her.

Mr. Quass laughed, looked at Grandpa and said, "Do you think we're ever going to find our money?"

"When I talked to my broker, he reassured me the stock market* would be closed for only two days. Let the panic calm down," said Grandpa.

"I couldn't get through to my broker, tried

all day Tuesday and Wednesday. Never did talk with him directly, just helplessly listened to the radio knowing shares were dropping and my fortune dwindling. It's all gone now," said Mr. Quass.

Grandpa nodded, "My shares are worth nothing now."

"Save a bed for me in the poor house," Mr Quass said.

"The poor house?" asked Hibbard.

"No one is moving to the poor house," Grandpa said laughing, looking at his pocket watch.

Marian looked up to Grandpa and then Hibbard. Hibbard raised his eyebrows. He heard it too. Grandpa's laugh was just like Mother's when she was nervous.

"When we go, let's take our curtains, Dear. They are so lovely," said Mrs. Quass.

The adults all laughed as they entered the home. Marian didn't understand the joke.

Mother turned from frying the chicken, hugged Grandma tight and didn't let go for a moment. When Mother released Grandma, she looked her straight in the eyes and they talked in hushed tones. Marian couldn't hear. But Mother gasped and covered her mouth. She gave Grandma another hug as Grandpa cleared his throat. Marian came over and hugged Mother. She gave Marian the salt and pepper shakers, gently pointing to the table. Marian climbed up onto her chair but watched her mother as she set the shakers at the center of the table. She stretched across the table to put a fork that fell off its napkin back in its place.

"How's your carving, Little Hib?" asked Grandpa, changing the subject.

Marian jumped down from her chair,

"Brubby, show Grandpa the dog you carved."

Hibbard ran into the next room where Mother, Daddy, Marian and he slept. When he returned, he held in his hand little carvings of a dog, a chicken, and a squirrel. They oohed and ahhed.

"These are wonderful," said Grandpa.

"He's going to be an artist," said Marian.

"They look like they might come alive," said Mrs. Quass.

During dinner all the talk was about money and the stock market. Marian tried to make sense of what they were saying. There was a bear* and a bull* at this market. Who would let those big animals in a market? And something crashed. Marian wondered if the bear crashed into a bull or the other way around. Marian had lots of questions, but she knew better than to interrupt the adults to ask. She would ask Hibbard later.

Sunday dinners were always filled with easy laughter when Mr. and Mrs. Quass visited, but this Sunday was different. Laughter seemed forced and nervous. Usually everyone sat comfortably in the chairs, but this Sunday everyone looked ready to spring up to do some imagined chore. Mr. Quass fiddled with his silverware which annoyed Grandpa. Mrs. Quass talked more than usual. Marian watched Mrs. Quass in fascination. Her words flew so fast Marian did not see Mrs. Quass even take a breath. One idea rolled into another in an endless stream.

When everyone finished eating, Hibbard and Marian jumped up to clear the table so Mother would serve the pie. Grandma turned on the coffee percolator and Mother placed the pie in the center of the table. Marian climbed up on her chair kneeling but sat on her bottom when Mother gave her a look. Marian had been eyeing the pie since yesterday. The meringue poofed up like a golden mountain, the crust just a shade darker, and Marian knew the lemon filling would be perfectly sweet with just a hint of tartness. Mother cut big slices for the men, medium slices for the women, and small ones for Marian and Hibbard. No one could bake pies like Mother. The children gobbled down their lemon meringue slices and then Hibbard asked to be excused. Mother had barely finished answering when the children were out the door.

Hibbard led and Marian followed. They didn't even plan to play Follow the Leader. They knew each other so well they just started. Around the lemon tree, through the pampas grass, along the chicken coop, over the stump, up onto the goat shed, and then Hibbard jumped down. When Marian climbed to the top, she was in such a hurry to catch up with Hibbard that she stepped off, tumbled down, crashing to the ground.

She heard Hibbard yell for help, and when Marian opened her eyes, there was Hibbard right by her side. Encircling her and leaning down were Mother, Daddy, Grandma, and Grandpa. They all looked very concerned. For a moment time stopped. She lay on her back and looked up into a circle of love. She tried to reach for her mother, but pain made it impossible to move her left arm.

"Oh Dolly, it looks broken," said Grandma.

"What were you doing up there?" asked Mother.

Not wanting to get Hibbard in trouble, Marian said, "Nanny Goat jumped up there."

"Sis, you're not a goat," chuckled Daddy.

"You've got to be more careful," said Mother.

Marian's tears moistened her cheeks. She wanted to linger surrounded by people that loved her and she loved back. For that moment, nothing existed outside that circle. She felt safe.

A New Friend

Marian was fighting the gritty Santa Ana winds,* which were full of feathers, sand, papers, and leaves flying past her. There had been no winds in the morning, so Marian hadn't brought the cap Mother had made for her. She knew without the cap covering her ears, she would have earaches tonight. She covered her ears with her hands as she leaned into the wind and pushed forward. Hibbard and his friend Rick had run on ahead and probably were already home.

Walking through the vacant lot Marian saw a clump of green that looked like Daddy's old army coat. When she got close she saw a man hunched over, his head rested on his knees and his coat pulled around him.* Marian looked for Hibbard, but he was out of sight, so she walked up to the man and asked,

"Hey Mister, are you all right?"

He sat up, his back to the wind, "Just a little hungry."

"Don't you have any food?"

"Not today."

"You haven't eaten anything, all day?"

"Nah uh."

"We've got food. Mother says you gotta eat whether you like it or not. Come on," Marian took his big hands in hers, "our farm's just over there on the corner of Juniper and Baseline."

Marian began jabbering on, "I have an older brother, Brubby. Well, really his name's Hibbard but I call him Brubby because when I was little that's what I called him and it just stuck. He's really good at 'Anty Over,'* he never drops the ball when it is thrown over the roof, and he throws it where he thinks I am on the other side of the shed. We play it every recess at school. Rick tags me all the time. He's so unfair. So when it was time for lunch recess, I jumped rope with Doris and Barbara Dell. They know how to play fair. But then the winds started up, and we all had to go in. You'll like my brother. He usually walks home with me but today he and Rick ran ahead. He doesn't like to be out in the wind because of his asthma. It's not good for him. He starts wheezing. He's really good at climbing trees. Do you like to climb trees?"

"It's been a while since I've climbed a tree."

"We've got a lot of trees on our farm. Do you like stories? Mother is reading us a story Aunt Mildred sent us for Christmas. It's the only good thing about going to bed at night — stories. It's called 'Hans Brinker or the Silver Skates.' Hans

and his sister, Gretel, are really poor, and sometimes they don't have any food, either. Some parts are really sad. They are getting ready for a skating contest, and whoever wins will get a brand new pair of shiny silver skates. I hope the mean girl doesn't win. We're rooting for Hans and Gretel. Have you read the book? Do you know who wins? No, no! Don't tell me, I want to be surprised. Here's our farm."

They walked up the long gravel driveway, and as they approached the house, Marian could smell Mother's cooking, "Oh, it smells like Mother is baking bread." She and her new friend walked into the kitchen. Mother stirred a big pot on the stove, her back to the door.

"Marian, what took you so long? Hibbard's already eaten a snack and started his homework."

"I met a friend."

Mother turned around, startled to see a dirty stranger standing in her kitchen. She reached over and pulled Marian to her.

"I don't mean any harm, Ma'am."

"He's hungry. He hasn't eaten anything all day."

Mother was silent for a moment staring at the stranger.

Marian said, "In Sunday School, Mrs. Ingold

told us, 'Happy are those who give food to the hungry.'"

Mother looked back at the stranger and then smiled at Marian, "Hibbard, move your books over and let this gentleman sit down. Marian, go get your father." Mother reached over to the percolator and poured the man and Daddy a cup of coffee without taking her eyes off the stranger.

When Marian returned with Daddy, her friend was eating a piece of pie and drinking coffee. He stood up when Daddy walked in, but Daddy waved him to sit back down.

"Ooo, can I have dessert before dinner?" asked Marian.

The adults laughed.

"Where were you stationed?" asked Daddy.

The stranger looked surprised, but then looked down and realized he had on his green wool coat. Only men who had fought in the Great War* had them.

"France. I was a private with the 165th Infantry."

"165th? Were you there during the Rouge Bouquet bombardment?"*

"Yes sir, with the Fighting 69th Regiment."

"Terrible day."

"Yes sir. You?"

"Puerto Rico, Second Lieutenant at Camp Las Casas in Santurce, San Juan — training soldiers."

Mother stirred a big pot of soup on the stove and took out two loaves of bread from the oven. She asked, "Do you have a family?"

"Yes, Ma'am. My wife and son are staying with her sister in San Francisco until I can find work."

"How old is your son?"

"Just turned six."

Marian jumped up. "I'm six, too."

"I thought so," said her friend.

"Marian, go get a half dozen eggs. And Hibbard, we're almost out of milk."

Marian ran out and Hibbard followed. The chickens squawked their disapproval of the wind as Marian searched for six eggs. She saw Hibbard trying to milk Nanny Goat, who was not cooperating. The wind tossed her about and pushed her back into the house. A gust threw open the door, and she almost dropped the basket of eggs. Mother washed the eggs, put them in boiling water, and Marian sat to listen to her friend talking with Daddy.

"We lost our farm waiting for that bonus

check* to arrive," said Marian's friend.

Whenever Daddy met a veteran, they started talking about the bonus checks. Marian heard all about it. It was a chunk of money that the government owed veterans for their service during the Great War. But the government didn't have to pay until the 1940s, and that was still nine years away. Veterans all over the country were out of work and needed it now.

"That bonus check would make our life a lot easier."

"Yes sir, but President Hoover vetoed the Veterans Bill in February. My brother-in-law said that's the end of that."

"Maybe. Ever hear of a fellow by the name of Waters, Sergeant Walter Waters?"*

"No, can't say I have."

"He's up in Oregon, somewhere," said Daddy. "He's speaking out at rallies up there. Says we need our money now."

"Hmm. Wish I could wait for speeches to do some good, but my family needs food today."

"Where are you going from here?" asked Daddy.

"I'm heading to Nevada, sir. My brother-in-law said they're starting a big dam project* near Las Vegas, looking for men who aren't afraid to work in 120-degree temperatures."

"What are they hiring for?"

"Right now they're looking for carpenters to build houses for the all the workers."

"You a carpenter?"

"I am, when my family's hungry. I figure I can build houses better than the tents and cardboard boxes they're living in now. My pa and I fixed whatever broke around the farm. You need anything done around here?"

"No, we're fine. I can take care of it. How many are they hiring?"

"Hundreds now, but when they start on the dam probably thousands. Once I get hired, I'll move my family out there."

Hibbard walked in wheezing with the milk bucket, looking mad at the goat, at the wind, at everything. Mother put a bowl of chicken soup, fresh bread and goat's milk in front of Marian's friend. He stopped talking and slumped over the bowl shoveling the soup into his mouth. Marian thought he must be really hungry. Maybe he didn't eat yesterday either. When he stopped eating and looked up, Marian's whole family was staring at him. He looked down,

"I'm sorry, Ma'am. It's just been so long since I've had a real meal. And it tastes so good.

Thank you. You sure I can't do any work for you, sir?"

"No. Thanks, though."

"It's a long way to Nevada," the stranger said standing up.

"Good luck to you," Daddy said as he shook his hand.

Mother filled a sack with a quart jar of soup, hard-boiled eggs, and her homemade bread. Marian put on a sweater and cap, ran outside, and picked an orange for the bag too. Daddy walked the man down to the road, Marian skipping behind. Daddy shook his hand, and then Marian's friend headed east on Baseline Road. Marian climbed up the eucalyptus tree as high as she could go, hung on tight and watched her friend get smaller and smaller in the wind until she couldn't see him anymore.

Eucalyptus Playground

The eucalyptus trees, originally planted as a wind break for the Santa Ana winds, provided the children with a playground. From their perch in the trees, Marian and Hibbard spied on the Basque sheepherders* across Baseline Road or Mother working in the chicken coop or Daddy pruning the orange grove. They used the eucalyptus pods for play money, pretend food, or balls to chuck at each other. The leaves woven together became crowns. Branches transformed into canes, scepters, and batons. And they climbed and explored every eucalyptus tree in the two rows that outlined their ten-acre farm.

One of Marian's favorite games was to climb a eucalyptus tree up and up until she could go no higher. She looked across to Hibbard in the next tree and smiled in anticipation. Then a quick check to make sure Mother was not watching. Mother saw danger everywhere. And, when all was safe, Marian and Hibbard each clung to their tree limbs, pushed away from the trunks and swung on their branches all the way down. The branches bent, dropping Marian and her brother on the ground giggling, and then sprang back into place.

One day Marian said, "Look how this bark rolls up."

"Looks like Daddy's cigarettes, only bigger like a cigar," said Hibbard.

"I wonder if they taste as good as they smell."

"One way to find out."

Marian peeked back at the house, "If Mother finds out, we'll get in big trouble."

"So we can't get caught. I'll get matches and find a good hiding place. You get the cigars ready."

Hibbard ran toward the goat's pen, along the length of the chicken coop to the end and slipped into the house. Marian tore the dried eucalyptus leaves as small as Daddy's tobacco in the Prince Albert tin. She rolled the cigar and waited. She knew Hibbard would find the best hiding place.

Hibbard ran back to Marian and said, "I found a place where no one will find us."

"Where?"

"Come on."

Hibbard took Marian to the other side of the chicken coop. A tarp hung from the roof of the coop over a stack of hay. They ducked behind the tarp. Hibbard was so smart. No one would see them behind the tarp.

They climbed the haystack and pulled the tarp down. Marian giggled and Hibbard shushed her. Hibbard reached under his shirt and pulled out a box of matches. Marian held out the eucalyptus cigar. With a very serious expression Hibbard struck the match and lit the cigar, inhaling. Immediately he started coughing and shoved the cigar at Marian. Always ready to follow her brother, Marian inhaled. She felt the smoke burn her throat, and she began hacking too. She couldn't get the cigar out of her hand fast enough. Hibbard had to take it back; he had started this. Marian wiped the strong eucalyptus smoke out of her eyes and watched Hibbard's face contort as his puckered lips kept the cigar at a distance. He puffed and coughed. Marian coughed more, thinking she had never tasted anything so wretched, but she couldn't be the one who backed out. She was handing the cigar back to Hibbard, feeling sick, when she heard footsteps on the other side of the tarp.

"Hibbard, someone's out there."

"Shhh!"

"Hey, what's going on back here?"

They froze. They had been caught. Daddy pulled down the tarp and snatched the cigar out of Hibbard's hand in a single move.

Marian didn't know whether it was the smoke or the coughing that had gotten Daddy's attention. But whatever it was, Daddy had come. Sure a spanking followed, but at least she didn't have to finish that eucalyptus cigar.

Daddy didn't give many spankings, but when he did, you didn't forget. Marian's tears were because the spanking hurt but also because she had disappointed Daddy. At first Marian thought Daddy was just mad, but then it seemed he was more scared.

"I'm doing everything I can think of to save our farm and then you two try to burn it down."

"Daddy, we didn't mean to...."

"One spark! One spark on that haystack, and the whole thing could have gone up in flames. And you two with it!"

Marian wanted to say she was sorry, but Daddy stomped off, and Marian thought it would be best to be quiet. For the rest of that day, Marian stayed out of the way and out of sight. She kept drinking water and wiping her tongue trying to get that awful taste out of her mouth. At dinner, Daddy talked calmly to Hibbard. "I'll be leaving in a week, Son. I need the three of you to be safe while I'm gone."

"We will be safe, Daddy. I promise."

"Boulder Dam is too far. If I'm hired, I can't be going back and forth like I did at the San Gabriel Dam."

"You won't have to, Daddy."

"I need you to protect your sister and help your mother. I need you, Son."

"Don't worry, Daddy. You can count on me."

Daddy paused, looked Hibbard in the eyes for a long time. Then he smiled, ruffled Hibbard's hair and said, "I know. I know I can."

Trains, Cookies, and Tinsel

Inside, Mother prepared the baking supplies and Daddy moved furniture for the tree.

Outside, Marian and Hibbard played with last year's Christmas gifts. Aunt Mildred had given Hibbard a Lionel electric train set. With only two small rooms in the house, there was no place to set up the tracks. So Hibbard put together the tracks of his Lionel train set outside in the sandy dirt. All year it was in a constant state of construction. Ramps, bridges and tunnels were built, then destroyed by the Santa Ana winds and vigorous play. Marian loved to play with the train as much as Hibbard. This year she hoped she might get a car or truck or train like her brother. Last year she had received the most beautiful doll she had ever seen, a Patsyette* doll, but she still would have preferred a truck.

Marian set up a small table and chairs by the chain link fence around the weir irrigation box at the corner of their property. Mother gave her a tablecloth and doll-sized napkins. Hibbard helped her hang curtains on the fence and carved a mirror, comb, and some dishes for the dolls. The two of them had tea parties with Patsyette and

Baby Doll, feeding them cut up mint and sugar. They never talked about the tea parties at school or when Rick Smith came over. But when it was just the two of them, Hibbard patiently played. Hibbard was Marian's best friend, and she was his faithful shadow.

As Hibbard fed Baby Doll and Marian fed Patsyette, the mail truck pulled into their driveway, but the children barely noticed, for they were having too much fun. Hibbard suddenly dropped the spoon, reached behind him, and grabbed a train car in each hand. He stretched his arms out as wide as he could and made the sounds of the Santa Fe line chugging down the track. The two trains, one in each hand, headed for each other. The chugging became more deliberate as the trains made their way down the imaginary track. Marian no longer fed Patsyette and watched Hibbard with sheer delight.

As the conductors in each train saw the impending disaster they blasted their whistles and screeched on their brakes. It was too late. Marian gasped for effect. The trains were so close, nose to nose. The children's voices collided with great crashing, banging, booming, and exploding. The train cars flew out of Hibbard's hands in different directions. Hibbard fell to the ground in slow

motion. He lay on his back with eyes closed and tongue hanging out of his mouth. Marian leapt up and ran to Hibbard who moaned. Marian grabbed a doll's blanket, dipped it in tea and dabbed Hibbard's forehead. Hibbard squinted his eyes with great effort and asked, "Where am I?"

"Fontana."

"What happened?"

"There's been a terrible accident."

Hibbard rolled on his side and "tried" to get up, "My family. Where's my family? I've got to find my family."

Marian looked at the table and knocked it over, sending the dishes, food and dolls flying. "We'll find them. Don't worry!"

"Are they still alive? Is there any sign of them?"

"We'll find them."

The children crawled under, around, and over the rubble of the crash.

"Look! I found Patsyette's hat. She must be over here!"

"We've got to find her!"

Hibbard crawled to Marian dramatically. In his search, Hibbard tried to remove the table but paused as if in pain; Marian came over and lifted the table.

"Look, she's still alive!"

Grabbing a doll napkin, Marian made a sling for Patsyette's arm and another became a head wrap. The mail truck slowly drove down the driveway and turned back on Baseline Road. Mother called. Marian and Hibbard ran up to the house, Patsyette still in Marian's arms.

"What happened to Patsyette?" Mother asked.

"She got in a train wreck," Marian said.

"Is she all right?"

"She will be," Hibbard answered.

"Oh good. Look what came in the mail."

"Oooh, Christmas presents!" squealed Marian.

"Maybe," Daddy said, "or maybe it's just an empty box."

"It's too heavy to be empty."

"Oh, it must be the farm tools I ordered."

"Nah! It's from Aunt Mildred."

"How did she know I needed tools?" Dad asked.

The children laughed and opened the box. There were two gifts, one for Marian and one for Hibbard. She closed her eyes and hoped for a truck. She shook it, squeezed it, smelled it. Mother laughed. "Put it under the tree, Marian."

"I just wanted to know what it is."

"Christmas is still a few days away."

"I can't wait."

Mother laughed, "Why don't you help me bake some jam cookies*?"

"Oooh, yum!"

Skipping over, she climbed onto the stool beside Mother, who rolled out dough while Hibbard played carols on the piano. After filling his coffee cup from the percolator on the stove, Daddy settled back in his chair to continue reading the latest issue of National Geographic. Mother cut circles out of the dough and Marian followed with the golden thimble to press out smaller circles from the center of every other one. Mother put a dab of loganberry jam on the large circle and then placed a circle with a doughnut hole on top. She pinched the sides and slipped the cookie sheet of treats in the oven. Mother let Marian eat the tiny leftover thimble circles. Marian sprinkled them with sugar and fed them to Daddy and Hibbard. A warm sweetness filled the air.

The tree that Daddy had brought home stood by the piano, making the room smell like a forest. Marian peered in a box of delicate glass ornaments on the table.

"Come on, Brubby, let's decorate the tree," said Marian.

Mother took Hibbard's place at the piano while the children sang and searched for the perfect spot to hang each glass ornament. On the boughs, they clipped small candle holders with candles.

From the bottom of the box Hibbard picked up a slender package wrapped in discolored tissue paper. Marian and Hibbard shared a glance. They knew what was in the package — strands of tinsel, hundreds, thousands, maybe hundreds of thousands. Each strand was saved from one year to the next, carefully stored on the cardboard, and wrapped in tissue to prevent tangling. Putting each individual piece of tinsel on the tree in the anticipation of Christmas wasn't so bad. But taking the tinsel off the tree strand by strand was an endless task, after all the other Christmas cheer had been packed away. The tinsel drove them crazy, taking each strand off, laying it on the cardboard, smoothing it out, and then threading each shimmering strand through the cardboard slot. Both children groaned.

Marian whispered, "Let's not put on the tinsel."

"Mother loves the tinsel."

"Then, let's put some on, but not all."

"Mom will know."

"Maybe not."

After the children decorated the tree, they called, "Look, Mother! Isn't the tree beautiful?"

"Oh my, yes!" The whole family sang "Oh, Christmas Tree" together. Mother got up from the piano to check on the cookies, but something she saw on the tree made her stop. Hibbard and Marian looked at each other hoping Mother hadn't noticed. Mother walked over and moved a couple of ornaments. "Come to think of it, the tree looks a little shy of tinsel. Don't we have any more?"

Daddy looked up from his reading, looked at the tree, Mother, and then the children.

Marian paused, wishing she could make the tinsel disappear. Reluctantly, she reached in the box and took out the cardboard with the remainder of the tinsel. "Here's some more."

"Oh good. Finish the job; you don't want to leave things half done."

Hibbard gave Marian an I-told-you-so look.

"You want to finish the tree, especially the tinsel," continued Mother.

"Why, especially the tinsel?" asked Hibbard.

"Because of the spider."

"What spider?" Marian asked, examining the

tinsel for spiders.

"I'm sure I told you about the Christmas Spider."

The children shook their heads.

"My grammar school teacher told me that when she was growing up in Germany, she heard a story about a kind old woman who was very poor. She lived by herself in a little cottage in the forest. Her only visitors were the animals. Through the cold, hard winter, she fed those animals. And each year in the days leading up to Christmas, she brought an evergreen tree into the house to decorate with fruits, nuts and cookies. Christmas morning, she took the tree to her animal friends as a gift.

"One year the spiders in her rafters decided to give her a gift. The most beautiful thing they had were the webs they could weave; so, while the old woman slept they went to work giving her the best that they had. When she awoke in the morning, she gazed upon the tree, clapped her hands, threw back her head, and laughed a hearty laugh. When she gazed upon that tree, she did not see sticky spider webs but instead saw shimmering strands of gold and silver."

"How did the spider web change to gold and silver?" asked Marian.

Mother paused and thought for a moment and then said, "That's a very good question."

Marian's eyebrows furrowed as she looked at the tinsel in her hands and then watched Mother walk back to the piano. Daddy smiled and looked down at his reading. Marian and Hibbard sang as they finished decorating the tree with every remaining strand of tinsel.

Shaking Earth

Hibbard had laid out the challenge — a race from the house zigzagging through the orange grove to the double row of eucalyptus trees at the back of the orchard, scrambling up a tree, swinging down from the highest branch, then back through the orange trees to the house. They each had a lane of trees.

Friday, March 10, 1933,* at 5:48 p.m.

"On your mark! Get set! Go!"

Hibbard shot off the starting line with Marian close enough to touch him. At top speed, they zigzagged through the orchard in five minutes. Marian reached the eucalyptus tree, and Hibbard was already past the first branch. She scrambled to get onto the first branch as Hibbard reached for the second. At 5:55 p.m. they felt it. Marian screamed and clung to her branch as it jolted to the left and then back to the right. Hibbard dangled upside down by his knees and one hand, grasping for a branch with the other. Hibbard righted himself as Marian shimmied down the tree.

"Golly Ned! What was that?"

Hibbard, bewildered, shrugged.

"Earthquake!! Hibbard! Marian! Where are you? Earthquake!"

Hibbard and Marian ran to their mother as the earth hiccupped under their feet. They paused, held out their arms for balance, and when the ground stopped shaking, they started running again. The oranges swung on the branches from side to side. The three of them huddled in the door frame of their house. Mother hugged the frightened children. Marian thought that the hug was meant to reassure them, but Mother squeezed so hard Marian knew she was scared, too.

Marian wished Daddy was home. Then she would feel safe. But Daddy was away looking for work.

They perched on the edge of their chairs at dinner, ready to sprint to the door frame if the earth decided to tremble again. They did their evening chores with all their senses keenly awake, no longer taking the ground under their feet for granted. That night the three of them slept in Mother's bed, Mother in the middle with both children leaning in on either side.

"Mother, tell us about Puerto Rico," said Hibbard.

"Oh, you don't want to hear about Puerto

Rico, again."

"Please," said Marian.

"You've already heard all about it."

"Please, just until we fall asleep," said Marian.

"Oh, all right. I taught English in Mayaguez."

"No. Start when you are on the boat," said Hibbard.

"On the boat? That's when I met your father."

"Yeah, that's the beginning."

Mother laughed. Marian loved when Hibbard got Mother to laugh. "I suppose that is the beginning to you. Your daddy and I were on the same boat going down to Puerto Rico: I to teach English at a high school in Mayaguez and your daddy to train Puerto Ricans to be soldiers in the US Army. He had wanted to go to Europe, but they needed him at Camp Las Casas in Santurce, San Juan, Puerto Rico."

"What did he look like?" asked Marian.

"Your daddy was so handsome in his lieutenant's uniform."

"Daddy said he couldn't take his eyes off you."

"He found plenty of excuses to be near me, and he caught my attention by reciting poetry, a whole poem or maybe just one line. We started talking and getting to know each other. It was all very exciting. There had been several sightings of German U-boats, so we zigzagged through the Caribbean. At night we kept the boat completely dark to avoid detection, the stars overhead our only lights. Your daddy couldn't even smoke his cigarettes."

"He must not have liked that."

"We talked and talked. I thought when we arrived in Puerto Rico we would go our separate ways. We lived on opposite sides of the island. But whenever he had time off, he would come to visit, all through that year."

"And then one day the earth shook," said Marian excitedly.

"Yes, I was completely thrown off. Growing up in Ohio, I had never felt an earthquake* before. Right in the middle of our morning lesson, everything shook, the walls jolted, the roof cracked, the desks slid. Children sprang out of their seats, ran out the door, and I stood in front of an empty classroom. My students were gone. But then a student remembered me and came back for me. He hollered at me but was talking so fast I couldn't understand."

"So what did he do?" Marian said sitting up.

"He grabbed hold of my hand and pulled. He knew living on an island, surrounded by water, that a tidal wave could follow an earthquake. We had to get to higher ground. Not wanting to slow him down, I ran as fast as I could. He pulled me to run faster. Dozens of people ran past us. We came upon a mother with two babies in her arms and trying to pull a toddler along, too. Without even slowing down and without letting go of me, my student bent down and scooped up the toddler and kept running. When we got to the top of the hill, we stopped. That was as far as we could go. People murmured prayers and kissed medals on chains as we looked back toward the beach. Babies cried."

"What happened then?" asked Hibbard.

"We waited. And then slowly people started down the hill. I went to the school thinking we would continue the lesson, but no one came back."

Marian and Hibbard laughed.

"So what did you do?" asked Marian.

"I made my way through town stepping over rubble that littered the dirt roads. Finally, I arrived at a pile of stones that had been my home that morning. The door frame stood upright, around it crumbled stones, debris and dust. A friend's family pitched a tent and invited me to stay with them until my host family could rebuild."

"What about Daddy?" asked Marian.

"Well, Daddy, got a jeep and drove through cracked and detoured roads to my side of the island. He arrived after dark and immediately started sifting through the rubble of my old house until someone told him where I was staying. When he drove up to the tent where we were, that's when I knew we would get married."

"Yuck," the children giggled, rolling on the bed.

"All right children; it is time to go to sleep."

They each said goodnight and lay in the dark with their private thoughts. Marian thought about Daddy and wished he were home. Mother must have known because she reached over in the dark, gently hugged Marian and rubbed her back. Marian listened to the breathing of her brother and mother align. The uncertainty of the shaking earth earlier in the day was replaced with the rhythm of her family breathing together. As if listening to a lullaby, she fell asleep.

In a Split Second

"Grandpa, look out!" Hibbard screamed.

They all looked out the car window and saw a black truck barreling down the hill straight for them. Grandpa didn't have time to swerve out of the way. The next moment was filled with breaking headlights and crashing metal followed by bamboo rakes flying through the air and scattering all over the road. Grandpa's front right tire rolled on ahead.

Marian looked over to Grandma who was holding her head wincing, "Grandpa, I think Grandma is hurt."

"No, no, I'm fine. How are you, Dolly?"

"I'm all right," Marian leaned forward over the back of the front seat, "How are you up here?"

"Fine, fine. We're fine."

A man ran over to the car, "Are you hurt? I'm so sorry. It was my brakes. My foot was all the way down on the floorboard. My brakes didn't work."

This one event took a split second. And that split second would define what was possible and what was not for Marian's family for years to come. Grandma was not fine; she would never be without pain again.

Moving In

Mother had decided to get a California credential, so she could teach again. She loved teaching and the income would really help the family. California would not let her teach with her Ohio credential. While Mother attended Claremont College, Grandma took care of the children in Santa Monica. The ocean became their backyard. Grandma was a fabulous cook and Marian and Hibbard got to sleep in their grandparents' big bed.

But after the accident Mother withdrew from college to take care of Grandma. There was no health insurance, so visits to the doctor were an out-of-pocket expense. Grandpa's finances dwindled trying to care for Grandma. They had lost their savings in the crash when the banks closed three and a half years earlier. But they held on to property they owned in Bel Air, Beverly Hills, Santa Monica, and Fontana. Marian's grandparents were property rich and cash poor. Bit by bit they sold off properties to pay doctor bills. Then the burden of juggling mortgages and doctor bills forced them to walk away from other properties, until all they had left was the house where they lived in Santa Monica.

When the terrible earthquake shook Southern California on March 10, 1933, it caused property damage in Santa Monica where Marian's grandparents lived. That Sunday Marian's grandpa said, "The earthquake shook the chimney clean off our roof, and the walls are full of cracks. We could sure use Big Hib's skills to repair it."

"He went back to Boulder Dam to see if he could get hired as a carpenter on the project. If he gets hired, he won't be back for a couple months."

"A couple months?" asked Grandma.

"And it doesn't look like he will be home in time for harvest."

"I can help you with the harvest," said Grandpa.

For the first time Mother, Grandma, and Grandpa talked about living together to help each other. The grandparents would try to sell their house in Santa Monica. Grandpa could work the farm and Grandma could cook and take care of Marian and Hibbard while Mother worked at Fontana Packing House to bring in some money. Marian and Hibbard listened with enthusiasm. This was the best idea ever. Although Mother was a great baker, she wasn't the best cook, but every

meal that Grandma served was delicious. Their little chicken coop house was about to get cozier.

On moving day, Marian and Hibbard couldn't sit still, trying to help everyone and always feeling like they were in the way. Grandpa seemed irritable, and tears seemed right behind Grandma's eyelids. Grandma unpacked her floral curtains and asked Mother if she could hang them in place of the plain white ones Mother had up.

"Of course, this is your house now, too," said Mother.

Grandpa hired a couple of men to help them move because Daddy was still working on the dam. The men unloaded the bulky green couch and jockeyed it through the doorway. The room was already crowded and now with their grandparents' things there was little space to move. Marian thought it would be fun to all sleep in one room, but Grandma and Grandpa would sleep in the living room on their pull-out couch and the rest of the family in the bedroom. When the Victrola was put in the corner, Marian immediately selected Daddy's favorite record "La Golondrina"* (The Swallow), set the needle on the record, and turned the handle. Spanish singers filled the house with song as Marian thought of her father working so far from home. She danced around the boxes.

It wasn't long before Grandma and Grandpa settled in, and Marian couldn't remember when they didn't live with them. Grandpa worked the orchard, Grandma cooked, Mother worked at Fontana Packing House, the children went to school and everyone had their chores with the chickens.

On the day when Daddy returned home, Grandpa was in the orchard, Grandma in the chicken coop, Mother in the kitchen and the children in the cypress trees. Mother came outside and Daddy swung her around in an embrace. Marian and Hibbard dropped out of the trees and ran to him. As he walked in the house, he stopped and surveyed the living room. He said, "I didn't realize it was Sunday."

Mother laughed and said, "It's not Sunday."

"Your folks are here, it must be Sunday."

Marian and Hibbard announced what was already obvious, "They live here now."

"Oh, do they?"

"Yes, isn't that great?" said Marian.

"We needed help," said Mother.

"I don't need his help," snapped Daddy.

"All right, I needed help! It was too much for me, and you were gone. Besides after the accident, my mother needed my...."

"Are they going to build a house on their property across Baseline?"

"They had to sell it. Medical bills ate up everything they had."

Daddy opened the door to the bedroom and peered in, "Where do they sleep?"

"The couch opens into a bed."

"How long are they staying?"

"As long as they need a place."

"They are going to be here forever. Isn't that great?" said Marian.

"Great," said Daddy.

He walked into the bedroom and Mother followed shutting the door behind them. While Marian set the table, Grandma and Grandpa came in.

"Big Hib home?" asked Grandpa.

"Uh huh, he's talking to Mother in our room."

Hushed voices started to rise and then returned to a hushed tone again. Grandma glanced toward the bedroom, shot a look at Grandpa who was sitting at the head of the table and then busied herself at the stove. Grandpa looked at his pocket watch, got up and pulled another chair to the table just as Daddy opened the door and walked over with Mother following. Grandpa stood back while Daddy reclaimed his seat at the head of the table. Mother sighed and brought the food to the table.

"Daddy, look what Grandma brought," Marian said pointing to the Victrola. "We can have music any time we want and she even has 'La Golondrina.'"

"Ah yes, about the tender swallow missing its home."

"Is that why you like the song so much because you missed us?" asked Marian.

"You bet, Sis."

"You are finally home so our family is complete," sang Marian to the tune of "La Golodrina."

Daddy seemed upset as he sang back "ya no puedo a mi masion volver."*

Mother, who was the only other one who understood Spanish, served Daddy and sang back, "Ave querida, amada peregrina, Mi corazón al tuyo estrecharé."*

Daddy's anger evaporated and they all celebrated his return.

Hog Ranch

Rumors circulated that thieves came to the country at night to steal from the farms, orchards, and ranches. Daddy had a guard dog by the name of "Lady," but there was nothing ladylike about that dog. Her sole purpose in life was to protect and defend, not the children, but Daddy. She was so serious about her job that she would not let anyone get close to him. Lady would growl at Mother if she hugged Daddy. Lady growled at Marian and Hibbard if they forgot and starting running toward their daddy. Lady was not allowed in the house so hugging was safe inside, but outside it was dangerous business. She never snapped or bit but her growl warned that she might.

The orange grove had been sold to Marian's family by the Fontana Farms Company, a development company that sold a grand scheme — better in theory than in practice. Even though they had food on the table every night, the family struggled to pay the mortgage. Daddy worked at the San Gabriel Dam, Boulder Dam and a variety of other jobs to help pay the mortgage bill.

When Fontana Hog Ranch* needed a night watchman to stop thieves from Los Angeles, Daddy was hired. During the day, Daddy worked in their own grove trimming, spraying, picking, fertilizing, and at night he went to the hog ranch where he made rounds to check on the hogs, armed with a gun, a lantern and Lady.

Each evening Mother and Grandma cooked an extra helping of dinner and brewed a thermos of strong, searing hot coffee to pack in his black domed metal lunch box. He started the truck as the sun went down and whistled for Lady to jump on the running board. Daddy, dressed in jeans, work boots and his fedora, drove four miles to the hog ranch while Lady sat tall, balancing on the running board.

Through the night he walked around the ranch checking on the hogs. To fight boredom between his rounds, he wrote poetry.* In the midst of the stink of the hogs and the darkness of the night and the danger of intruders lurking around the next corner, he created beauty. In the office was an old black Underwood typewriter. To the steady rhythm of Lady's breathing, Daddy pounded away on the typewriter keys. Tap. Tap. Click, Click, Click. Tap. Tap,Tap,Tap. Clack, Clack. Click, Click, Tap, Tap, Tap. Ding. Ratchet, kchkchkch, shshshshshshhs. Tap, Tap, Tap....

After twenty minutes of creating he pushed

his chair away from the desk. The metal legs scraped across the concrete floor. With Lady at his side, he walked through the muck and mud counting every hog. They grunted, shifted their weight, lifted their heads as his lantern shown over their backs and into the corners. After about forty minutes in the labyrinth of pens Daddy was back at the office door stomping the mud out of the crevices of the soles of his work boots before walking in. He opened the thermos with a sthhh/ swosh and poured steaming black coffee into the cup and for just a moment the richness of the coffee overpowered the smell of the hogs. He leaned back in this chair and re-read the words he had left in the typewriter cradle. All night long, he drifted back and forth between two worlds.

Every morning Mother greeted Daddy at the door with a plate of eggs, fresh baked bread and steaming black coffee. One morning as Mother was cutting oranges at the counter, Daddy slipped in beside her and dangled a shimmering spoon in front of her. Her eyebrows raised, and she took hold of a delicate sterling silver grapefruit spoon, spinning it between her fingertips and then wiping it on her apron.

"It was almost completely buried in the muck, just the tip poking out," Daddy said, looking over Mother's shoulder. "Can you believe someone wouldn't know they were throwing away silver?"

"Shouldn't we return it?" Mother questioned.

Daddy chuckled, "To whom? Do you want me to go door-to-door in Beverly Hills and ask, 'Are you missing a spoon?' Besides the boss said we could keep anything we found in the pens."

The hogs of Fontana ate the garbage from rich Los Angeles neighborhoods. Six hundred tons of garbage was sent by railroad daily to feed them. Sometimes as a servant or waiter scraped plates into the garbage, an odd piece of silver would slip into the garbage with the slop. After that first treasure arrived home, Marian couldn't wait to see what other treasures Daddy might uncover in the hog pens.

Marian loved waking to the sounds of Daddy's truck tires grinding down the gravel driveway and Mother puttering in the kitchen.

But one Saturday morning, Daddy wasn't home when Marian got up. A plate of eggs was on the stove getting cold. Mother, a worrier, talked about one possible scenario after another explaining why Daddy was so late. By the time Daddy did get home, she had imagined he had fallen, gotten in a car crash, been stepped on by a hog, attacked by a wild animal. He had been hurt, maimed, left for dead, and even died — at least once. So hearing the tires on the gravel road this morning was a huge relief.

Marian was the first one out the door but Hibbard and Mother were right behind. Lady stepped off the running board and limped to the side of the chicken coop. The family swarmed around Daddy with questions as they walked in.

Daddy told his story.

It had started as a normal stinky, dirty Friday night on the hog ranch. He took his breaks in the office at the typewriter pounding out poetry. At 4:30 a.m. Daddy pushed away from the typewriter, frustrated that he couldn't find the right word. His mind was still in the office ruminating over the poem that lay cradled in the typewriter. He opened a door in an out-building, and Lady sounded the alarm. Her blackish-brown fur bristled and she growled a deep throaty growl that erupted into a bark. She lunged out of the scope of the light.

Hearing a man holler and bump into the wooden pens, Daddy lifted his lantern. It sounded like Lady was tearing someone apart. Daddy ran after Lady with his gun drawn, ready to shoot the intruder. As he held up the lantern, it bounced with

each step, but he caught sight of a man in overalls running in one direction while looking back over his shoulder at the dog. The light illuminated the blade of a machete.

"If Lady hadn't been with me, the man probably would have killed me with that machete."

"Kill you?" asked Marian.

"A hungry man doesn't hide behind a door with a machete unless he's planning on using it."

The family encircled Daddy, squeezing him tight. Mother cried over everything and this was no exception.

"Come on, let's find Lady," said Hibbard.

The children ran out toward their heroine. Lady lifted her head and growled with her back fur bristling. The children stopped. How could such a good dog be so mean?

Violin Recital

Marian put the violin under her chin, dragged her bow across the strings to squeak, squeal and screech her way through tunes. Miss Turner, Marian's violin teacher, was always very encouraging, and Marian's mother and daddy supported her, but Marian thought she sounded terrible. The animals started bleating, howling, and clucking when she played. Mother said they were singing, but Marian thought they were begging her to stop.

Every few days, Mother baked and sold thirteen pies to pay for Marian's violin lessons: lemon meringue, raspberry, loganberry, apple, boysenberry, blueberry, coconut cream, banana cream and cherry. If the fruit was in season, Marian and Hibbard picked it. If not, Mother bought the fruit canned. Mother made the best pies in town, and Marian loved pie-making days.

Daddy built a wooden crate with thirteen pie shelves and a handle on top. Mother filled the pie rack and drove to a small restaurant called Gingham Gal. It was a little white bungalow with gingham curtains and waitresses dressed in gingham aprons. When Marian went to deliver the pies with Mother, she looked around and wondered what it was like to eat at a restaurant.

Mother put the money from selling the pies in a jar in the kitchen. Every Saturday for a year she dipped into that jar to pay Mildred Turner, Marian's violin teacher. "Pies for music," she said.

On the last Saturday of the school year Miss Turner announced that there would be a recital at the end of August at the Women's Club. In just a few short months Marian would have to play for an audience — in front of people other than her family and teacher. This didn't sound like such a good idea. The Fontana Women's Club had a big, beautiful stage with heavy curtains. Chandeliers hung from the ceiling, and arched windows surrounded the building. People regularly came to the club for luncheons, musical concerts, and movies. It was a fancy place, and Marian wondered if her playing was good enough.

"Practice, practice, practice," said Daddy.

"What will you play?" asked Hibbard.

"Miss Turner said everyone will have two pieces, one solo and one duet. She wants me to play 'The New Doll' by myself and the 'Cradle Song' with Carolyn," Marian said.

"Those are lovely pieces," said Mother.

"You play them well," said Hibbard.

"Miss Turner said we have to have the tunes memorized."

"You'll get it. I can help you practice if you want," said Hibbard.

That summer Hibbard did help Marian practice, he playing the piano and she the violin. Note by note, measure by measure, line by line, she learned the pieces by heart. Every week when Marian met with Miss Turner, the teacher applauded Marian's progress. As the end of the summer drew near, she felt ready. Daddy and Mother were excited about the recital. One night at dinner Daddy said, "Tomorrow we're going shopping in San Bernardino at Harris Brothers."

Marian sat upright with a sparkle in her eye. Harris Brothers was a magical place. With three floors and an elevator to ride up and down, it was an explosion of activity — so much to see there. "What do we get to buy?"

"A dress," said Daddy.

Marian thought Daddy was going to buy Mother a store-bought dress and wondered why.

"Someone needs a new dress for a recital," said Mother.

Marian gasped and leapt out of her seat. She ran over to Daddy, then Mother, and hugged them tight.

"Me? A store-bought dress for me?"

Mother had sewn all Marian's dresses from fabric she brought in her old trunk from Ohio. When Mother was growing up, Grandpa had hired dressmakers to sew all her dresses. Now those dresses lay in the trunk waiting to be refashioned by Mother's skillful hands into dresses for Marian or shirts for Hibbard.

Marian had never shopped for a dress before; she curtsied, twirled, and posed in one dress after another. Then Mother lifted a pink organdy dress off the rack. Marian squealed. It was dotted swiss with a lace collar, puffy short sleeves, and a bow that tied in the back.

"Let's try this one on," said Mother.

"Do you really mean it Mother? It is the most beautiful dress. Oh, Mother!"

"Let's hope it fits."

Marian was beaming when she walked out of the dressing room.

"Turn around, Marian. Let me tie the bow." Mother tugged at this seam and that, turning the hem over to see the width. "Marian, hold your arms up like you are holding the violin. Does that feel comfortable?"

"It feels perfect."

"Daddy, what do you think?"

"I think my daughter will be the most beautiful violinist on that stage. Let's get some white shoes to match."

"Shoes, too?"

"Well you can't wear your old oxfords with such a pretty dress."

When the store clerk asked about shoe size, Marian requested them a couple sizes big. And Mother corrected her, telling the clerk Marian's actual size.

"But Daddy always gets the shoes too big so we have growing room."

"Your feet are not going to grow in one week."

Usually Daddy bought the children's shoes too big, and then stuffed the toe with newspaper until the shoes fit. When the sole had a hole, they put cardboard between their feet and the ground. But when the sole had two or more holes Daddy got out his "cobbler's cast iron shoe form" and resoled the shoe and the children wore that pair until they no longer fit.

The night before the recital, Marian couldn't fall asleep. Long after the rest of her family was sleeping, she was staring at the ceiling, turning one way and then another, pulling the blanket up and covering her eyes. She rolled over, sitting up to fluff her pillow and lay back down. If she slept at all, she didn't know when because it seemed to her that she saw every minute of every hour.

Finally, a sliver of light shone in. Marian jumped up, put on her dress, tights, and shoes and sat on the edge of her bed waiting for the rest of her family to wake up. Mother laughed, "Marian, put on your play clothes, we'll go to the recital after an early dinner."

"I just want to be ready," Marian said.

"You're ready. Go back to sleep," said Hibbard and he rolled over.

"Marian, you don't want to get these clothes dirty. Come on. I need your help in the orchard," said Daddy. All morning Mother and Daddy took turns keeping Marian busy. After lunch, Mother filled the wash tub on the porch. She picked a Bella Portugal rose and sprinkled in petals for Marian to take a bath.

Marian fastened a white and pink flowered bracelet around her wrist, put on her slip and insisted on practicing her pieces. She played flawlessly from memory. After dinner she put on her dress, tights and shoes. She sat in the car with the violin on her lap. As Daddy started driving, Marian opened the case and made sure the bow hairs were loosened and her rosin was back in the case.

Upon arrival, Miss Turner whisked Marian backstage behind the big, heavy curtains. The piano sat in the center of the stage. Miss Turner struck the "A" on the piano and started tuning the violin. Marian peeked out from behind the curtains and saw Daddy, Mother and Hibbard sitting in wooden folding chairs looking so proud. Mother had worked hard so that her children could be classically trained. Hibbard had been playing piano for several years and now Marian was tuning up for her very first recital. Marian saw Mother beaming.

The curtains opened and Miss Turner stepped out to welcome and greet the audience. Marian started to feel sick. Halfway through the program, Marian was going to play a duet with her friend Carolyn, but first they each would have to play their solos. One of Miss Turner's older students, Jean, walked out on stage. She sat down at the piano and started playing "Barcarolle." Carolyn and Marian giggled and clasped each other's hands. They wanted to waltz, but Miss Turner shushed them. Then Carolyn watched her little sister play. She was so cute. Marian and Carolyn silently smiled at each other. After her curtsy she ran off stage and gave Carolyn a hug.

Carolyn picked up her violin and stood in the wings waiting for her turn until the teacher announced "Gavotte." Carolyn played so well, only squeaking a couple times. But the audience probably didn't notice the squeaking.

Marian rubbed more rosin on her bow. And waited. Her stomach started churning. She tried to push all sounds out of her head so her ears could remember the notes of her piece. She remembered the middle, but she couldn't remember how "The New Doll" started. What was the first note? She just needed to remember the first note. And then she heard her teacher announce "The New Doll" played by Marian Moore. Oh no, what was the first note? Maybe they wouldn't notice if she didn't go out. Jean walked over to Marian, smiled and whispered, "It's your turn." Marian's feet moved her onto the stage but her eyes lingered backstage, hoping, desperately hoping, somehow she would remember the first note. She looked out into the audience and spotted her Mother, Daddy and Hibbard smiling — Mother who had baked hundreds of pies to pay the violin teacher, Daddy who bought Marian the most beautiful dress in the world and shoes that fit, and Hibbard who encouraged and practiced with her until she felt confident — all smiling for this moment. She watched as their smiles sagged. Miss Turner chuckled nervously and announced Marian's piece again. Marian brought the violin up, the bow ready, but what was the first note? Daddy smiled at her, Mother nodded her head, and Hibbard looked like he wanted to yell, "You know this. You can do it." Marian heard people in the audience shuffle in their seats and clear their throats. Marian fought back the tears and desperately searched her memory for the starting note. She couldn't find it. She couldn't move. She just stared. Jean walked on stage and gently put her arm around Marian's shoulders and guided her off stage. Marian lowered her head, a tear dropped on her pink organdy dress and she watched her pretty white patent leather shoes walk off stage. The audience applauded politely.

Two sisters went on stage and played a duet. In a whisper, Miss Turner talked with Marian, while Jean rubbed her back, and Carolyn held Marian's hand.

"Honey, you usually play 'The New Doll' so well. What happened?" said Miss Turner.

"I forgot how it started, Then I got scared being out there all by myself," whispered Marian back.

"You must be a real performer, then. All of us get scared sometimes. Do you think you can go out there with Carolyn for your duet?"

Marian looked at Carolyn, whose eyes were pleading. Marian nodded.

"Good girl."

Miss Turner stepped onto the stage and introduced Marian and Carolyn playing "Cradle Song" by Brahms. Jean leaned down to the girls before they stepped on stage, smiled and whispered,

"It's in the key of C and the first notes are EEG, EEG, EGCBAAG."

The girls giggled and took center stage together. They played their duet without a squeak, squeal, or screech. Marian was relieved when it was over and she could walk off the stage. Everyone in the audience and backstage applauded loudly.

After the recital, all the parents congratulated the performers. Marian lingered in the back of the crowd but her family found her. Marian was fighting back tears. "I'm sorry I let you down," she said.

"Now mind, I'm proud of you," said Mother.

"But I forgot the first song,"

"It must have been scary on that big stage for the first time all by yourself," said Hibbard.

"I'm proud of how you rallied for the second piece," said Mother.

"I've never heard that played better," said Daddy wiping Marian's tears, "And you were the prettiest girl up on that stage tonight."

Secret Hideaway

When Marian and Hibbard dug in the abandoned field across Baseline Road, they were in Egypt or Africa or South America creating a secret hideaway — their own ancient ruin. They knew all about ancient ruins from their monthly subscription of the National Geographic Magazine. Even in the toughest times, they received the magazine; Aunt Mildred made sure of it because she knew how much Mother loved to look things up. The whole family would comb through the articles imagining a world beyond their Southern California orange grove. The abandoned field by the old dump was far enough away to be out of the sight lines of their parents and grandparents. The workings remained a secret so that it would be a place of their own. As long as they could keep it a secret, it belonged to them.

During the spring, the Basque sheepherders brought thousands of bleating sheep through the abandoned field. No one in Fontana wore clothes like them, and they spoke a language strange to the children's ears. When Marian and Hibbard heard the bleating and the tinkling of bells, they ran down to Baseline Road, and from their perch in the eucalyptus trees, they watched the sea of wool. Mother, always fearful, warned them to keep their distance or the strangers might steal them away and, of course, that danger made the sheepherders even more appealing. So every waking hour for the three days that the Basque sheepherders camped in the field, Marian and her brother stayed in the trees watching, wondering where they came from and where they were going, looking for stolen children, and trying to understand what they were saying to each other.

When the sheepherders left, Hibbard and Marian went excavating the camp site to see what clues they might have left behind. They found old bottles and metal scraps. While digging through the camp, they found a perfect spot for the ancient ruin on the side of the Muscat and Sweet Water grape vines that grew wild. During the last few weeks of spring, they discussed grand plans, revised them and decided. As soon as school got out for the summer, they started digging.

Daddy worked nights as a watchman at Fontana Hog Ranch, and then when he got home in the morning, he worked in the orchard a couple of hours while the children slept. When the light came on in the kitchen, Daddy would join Grandma there. Grandma mixed up some buttermilk dough. She rolled it, looped it over and then flipped the twisters* one after the other into the fat simmering on the stove. Daddy got out his famous watermelon syrup.*

The children awoke to the sweet smell and heard Daddy teasing Grandma, "Mother, why are we raising chickens? Forget the oranges too. We should open a shop: Twisters and Watermelon Syrup."

"They'd come from miles around," chuckled Grandma.

After breakfast, Marian and Hibbard cleared the table and Daddy slipped into the still warm bed. When he slept, Marian and her brother had to be out and away from the house, so they didn't accidentally wake him up. Mother and Grandpa went out to the chicken house while Grandma quietly cleaned up and then rested her back as she read the National Geographic on the couch. As Marian headed for the door, Hibbard grabbed an orange for each of them. Marian and Hibbard exchanged furtive whispers.

Keeping watch, they sprinted to the garage, slipped in and borrowed Daddy's shovel and screwdriver and loaded them into Hibbard's red racer wagon. Marian and he ran to Baseline Road pulling the wagon. They paused at the eucalyptus trees just to make sure no one was watching. Grandma stood outside the kitchen looking in their direction. They stood perfectly still. Smiled. Waved. Grandma waved back and hobbled over to the flowers and snipped some Bella Portugal roses. She paused at the door and looked back at Marian. She watched them watching her. Hibbard said, "Do something."

He climbed a tree and Marian dropped down on her knees as if digging in the dirt. Hibbard raised his head and Marian lowered hers. Grandma went inside, Hibbard dropped down and Marian stood up. They crept closer to Baseline, and when no one was watching, they dashed across the road to their site. Hibbard and Marian got to work filling wagons full of sand, dirt, and rocks.

Every day for weeks, they worked on their hideaway until it was big enough to stand up in. Getting in the hideaway was an easy jump; getting out was tough because once in, they had to pull themselves up and out. With a screwdriver, Marian carved stairs making it easier to climb out. They decided their ancient ruin needed a roof so travelers passing in the dark wouldn't fall in. They

dragged a large piece of corrugated metal over the top of the hole. From deep in the ground, Hibbard lit a match, melting wax into a can and stuck the end of a candle upright. The flickering candle cast shadows in their very own ancient ruin. Now that it was almost finished, they renewed their promises. They each solemnly pledged not to tell anyone about their secret hideaway.

Mother called for dinner, and they climbed up the stairs, pulled the metal roof into place and covered it with dirt. It was totally secret. No one would ever know it was there.

Or so they thought.

The next day Marian and Hibbard sat at the kitchen table antsy to finish breakfast and get outside to their special place. When they were done, they leapt up from the table. Daddy leaned back in his chair and rolled a Prince Albert cigarette. It was strange that Daddy had not gone straight to bed, but Marian noticed he had dirt all over his pants and must have been in the middle of a project in the orchard when the fritters were ready. They looked over their shoulders as they ran down to Baseline and then across the road to the field and their secret hideaway. But they were back before Daddy finished his cigarette. Marian and Hibbard burst through the door.

"They ruined it," Hibbard and Marian cried.

"It's all caved in."

"They destroyed it."

Marian looked around and everyone was still there. Grandpa fingered his pocket watch, Mother wiped the table, Grandma heated water on the stove for dishes and Daddy was still smoking at the table. He inhaled and asked, "What? Slow down, what's going on?"

"We dug an ancient ruin across the road and some big boys came along and smashed it," Marian explained.

"Ancient ruin?" Daddy said.

"It was big enough to stand up in," Hibbard said.

"Wow, that would have to be pretty big. Doesn't sound safe to me," said Daddy.

"It was even better than in the magazines. We dug and we dug. And now all our hard work is for nothing. For nothing," Marian cried.

Hibbard shook his head, "It's just a big heap of dirt."

"Why?" Marian said, "It's so unfair!"

"I'm glad you weren't in it when it collapsed," said Daddy.

Hibbard and Marian looked at each other

and then around the room. Daddy didn't understand. None of them did. Someone destroyed their hideaway and was getting away with it. Marian shook her head, disgusted. Realizing they would not get help from the adults, she and her brother ran back outside to gather evidence of the crime.

Hanging On

The oranges hung heavy in the grove. The limbs carried the weight of the harvest waiting to be picked.

Hibbard watered and fed the 2000 chickens while Marian raked down the chicken mash. Then they raced each other back to the kitchen. It was dinnertime for them too and they were hungry. The children stopped at the kitchen door and heard Daddy's and Grandpa's voices flaring.

Daddy barked, "They aren't buying. What do you expect me to do?"

"You have to try," Grandpa spat.

"Try? Try! I have! The packing houses aren't buying."

"You can't let the crop rot on the branches."

"The guard stopped me at the gate, wouldn't let any farmers through."

"It's common sense, if one method fails you try another. If the packing houses won't buy our oranges, then we must find someone who will."

"Who? Who has money for my oranges?"

Marian and Hibbard hated when Daddy and Grandpa argued. Daddy was a miner, not a farmer;

no one could have worked any harder to make the farm a success. But it wasn't. The farm always struggled and now they were in danger of losing the farm altogether. Grandpa had a lifetime of success: his farm in Ohio, a brick factory, and a real estate business. Until the accident, his life had been a steady stream of successes, but now Grandpa had lost everything and had to live at the end of a chicken coop. When Grandpa and Daddy looked at each other they saw their own failures, so they tried to avoid each other, but in their cramped space it was impossible. Tempers flared easily.

Everyone in the house knew how important this harvest was. For years the chickens had supported them as they worked and waited. This is what they had waited for, what they had worked for: this harvest. Just a couple more payments and Daddy would own the farm. The crop hung on the branches ready for harvest, but packing houses had stopped buying the oranges. The children swung open the kitchen door and silence crashed into the room. Mother turned her back not wanting them to see her tears. But they knew! It's what she always did. Mother cried, Daddy yelled, Grandpa stiffened and Grandma silently busied herself. The children washed their hands, sat down and looked around the table. Food was passed without a word. Everyone studied their plates. Marian kept her gaze down but peeked around the table — not moving her head — just her eyes. Hibbard did the same.

After dinner, Daddy pushed his chair away from the table and rolled a Prince Albert cigarette. He took a book of matches from his pocket, lit the cigarette and took a slow draw. Grandpa stood up as straight and stiff as a corn stalk, he adjusted his glasses, checked his pocket watch, and went outside. The children jumped up and secretly followed him.

He walked directly to his shiny, dark green Willys-Knight with leather interior and hickory wheels. Not a scratch, a dent, or a ding. He noticed a leaf on the hood and removed it. He got the tool chest from the shed, opened the back door to his car and crawled in to loosen nuts, bolts, and screws, carefully placing each piece of hardware in order on the ground beside the car. He banged, pried, pulled, and yanked, but the seat held on tight to the body of the car.

Hearing the commotion, Daddy came outside and watched for a moment in bruised silence. Grandpa looked up; they each stood firm on opposite sides of the car. A hundred unvoiced arguments shot between them. The children hid out of sight behind a rose bush. Grandpa struggled to pry the last bolt free. Daddy slowly took the tool from Grandpa and levered the seat loose. The children watched as the men's eyes softened, their shoulders rounded, and they gave in to lifting the back seat out — together. No words passed between the men. They each knew the next step. Walking to the side of the shed, each picked up a heavy crate of oranges and emptied the oranges into the back of the car.

Grandpa's leather back seat was now leaning against the side of the shed where the orange crates had been stacked and oranges filled the back of his car where the seat had been. Adjusting his tie, Grandpa walked inside saying, "We can't let the fruit rot without trying something."

For the next several weeks, early each morning, Grandpa and Daddy drove to Foothill Blvd. and sold oranges, three for five cents, out of the dark green Willys-Knight with hickory wheels and leather interior. The mortgage payment came due but couldn't be made.

The family's talk began to turn from how to save the farm to where they would go and what they could do. Daddy left again, searching for work in a time when no one was hiring. Preparations on the farm began for the eventual move. Hibbard and Marian picked berries, vegetables, and fruit for preserves. Mother and Grandma canned fruits and vegetables with a new urgency, uncertain about the future. And Grandpa dressed in a suit each morning and continued selling oranges from the back of his prized car.

After a few weeks, a huge flatbed truck drove up the long driveway blasting its horn. Marian and Hibbard high in the cypress trees hung upside down from the trees by their knees to see who had arrived with such fanfare. When they saw it was Daddy, they dropped down out of the trees and chased after the truck.

Wiping her hands, Mother ran out to greet him. Daddy picked her up and spun her around and exploded with the news. "I found a mine in the Mother Lode. A second boom, they say. Miners are needed who know what they are doing. I spoke up for a cabin, and my partner let me borrow his truck to move us all up to the mountains."

A short time after the harvest ripened and then rotted, the bank took the farm. The family had hoped to hang on. They had hoped the packing houses would start buying oranges again before their payment was due. They had hoped to stay on their farm. But now their hopes turned north to the Mother Lode. After all, Daddy was a miner, not a farmer.

Moving North

Mother listened to Daddy talk about mining with admiration. He knew all about geology, and when he talked, there was no doubt Daddy was going to strike it rich. Marian couldn't wait to see a real gold nugget. They just had to get there; the gold was waiting for them.

The house was a hub of activity. The whole family prepared for the move north: sorting, packing, cleaning, cooking, and canning.* Hibbard and Marian picked fruit or vegetables and Daddy prepared chickens for Mother and Grandma to cook and store in jars. When they moved, they would rely on what they could preserve. Daddy built a long slender box, like a coffin, to hold hundreds of glass jars of fruits, vegetables and meats.

The idea of mountain life seemed a little too rustic for Grandpa and Grandma so they decided to go live with Aunt Mildred in Oakland, at least until Marian's family got settled. Grandma asked Marian to take care of the Victrola for her. Marian loved dancing and singing with the Victrola. They also sent their couch to the mountains with Marian's family because Aunt Mildred had a bed for them.

On moving day, they packed the Buick with what they needed for the trip and the flatbed truck with what they would want or need in the years to come. In the truck was the couch, Victrola, beds, dressers, table, chairs, the box of 700 jars of food, piano, books, dishes, silver utensils, trunk of fabric, sewing machine, rug, tools, and boxes of clothes and belongings. Using every inch of space, they piled the furniture high. Tied to the end of the truck were two cages, one housing the milking goat and the other a half dozen chickens.

They got ready to say good-bye to their friends, the Eckfords, who lived right by the violin teacher. Each Saturday for the last year after the violin lessons, Mother stopped by to visit Gertie, and Marian got to play with her school friend, Barbara Dell, and her younger sister, Betty Lou. The Eckfords raised chickens and oranges, too, but they lived in a comfortable brick house. On moving day, Gertie, Gene, Barbara Dell, and Betty Lou came to say goodbye. Barbara Dell and Betty Lou jumped out of their car and gave Marian sweet hugs. They danced around each other, and the two friends promised to write. Barbara Dell leaned back in the car and pulled out a gift for Marian. Everyone watched Marian open it.

"It feels like my birthday," said Marian.

She opened the box to discover a red plaid store-bought dress. Mother or Grandma had sewn every one of her dresses except the pink organdy dress Daddy bought her for the recital. This was her second store-bought one. Marian hugged the dress to herself and twirled.

"I love it!"

Then she looked at Barbara Dell. She was wearing the same dress.

"We're twins," both girls chimed in together.

Giggling, the girls ran into the house. They emerged dressed alike and struck a pose like two bookends.

Marian asked, "Can we play hide and seek?"

"Not for long. We've got to get on the road," said Mother.

"Don't get dirty," said Gertie, looking at Barbara Dell.

Hibbard laughed, saying, "You two will be easy to find in those red dresses. You better find a really good hiding place."

"I'll go to the mountains to hide," said Marian.

"Underground? In a mine?" asked Hibbard.

"You'll never find me."

The children all laughed. The adults exchanged looks. The mountains were where their hopes were hiding. In the mine there was always the hope of finding gold, but above ground was the evidence of what they had lost. Mother took a deep breath, and Gertie gave her a hug. The two disappeared into the house. Daddy and Gene turned toward the truck and began talking about the knots that tied everything down. Hibbard covered his eyes and started counting. The girls squealed and ran.

Marian and Barbara Dell ran to the middle of the grove and hid behind trees. Barbara Dell's younger sister, Betty Lou, ran one row in and hid. Barbara Dell called to her sister and motioned her to come over. Betty Lou started running toward her but then all three heard Hibbard call, "Ready or not, here I come."

Barbara Dell and Marian disappeared behind the foliage of the trees and Betty Lou darted behind the nearest tree. Marian saw Hibbard run right at Betty Lou, and then past her into the middle of the grove. Barbara Dell and Marian hid behind neighboring trees. They held their breath, making faces at each other.

Daddy called, "Come on, we've got to get started. It's a long trip."

The girls silently counted on their fingers to three and leapt out on each side of Hibbard. He jumped. They all laughed and ran to the house.

With hugs and promises Hibbard, Hibbard's kitten, Midnight, and Daddy got in the truck; Marian got in the blue Buick with Mother. Daddy drove down the long driveway with Mother following. Barbara Dell ran along the Buick waving until they got to the end of the driveway. The Buick followed the truck turning northeast with a flurry of waving from the girls.

They drove all afternoon. As night fell, they arrived in Mojave and stayed in an auto court.* Daddy slept in the truck to guard their stuff while Mother, Marian, Hibbard and Midnight slept in the room. Hibbard milked the goat in the morning and met a girl who was staying in the auto court, also. The girl's family truck was piled high with furniture too. She played with the kitten as it tried to get some of the goat's milk that had spilt.

"You want my kitten?" asked Hibbard. "Her name is Midnight."

"Uh. We don't have any food for a cat."

"She's a really good mouser. Or she'll eat any leftover scraps."

"Sure. Why you gettin' rid of her?"

"My Pop says I have to."

The girl scooped up the kitten and ran back to her room, "Mommy, look what I got."

Marian asked, "Why did Daddy say you had to give away Midnight?"

"He said she was too wild in the truck."

"She's just a kitten."

"She scampered all over, from the back of the seat to the floor to the seat. I couldn't hold her still. When she scratched Daddy, I'm surprised he didn't stop right then."

"She scratched Daddy?"

"She didn't mean to, but Daddy pushed her off his lap."

"Oh, no."

"I wish I could have kept her calm."

"I'm going to miss her."

"Me, too," Hibbard said shaking his head.

Mother called to Marian and she ran over and got in the Buick. Continuing north, Mother drove the Buick slowly enough for Marian to see the flowers outside her window.

"Oh, there's a pretty one. Can you see that one there?" asked Marian.

"What's its name?" asked Mother.

"I don't know."

"Look it up. Look it up. You wouldn't want to be called 'That one there.' The flowers want to be called by their names."

Marian smiled and reached for the book

which was on the seat because she had already looked up Joshua tree several miles back. She flipped through the pages looking for a flower like the one she saw out the window. Mother drove slowly until steam rose up from the hood and she pulled over. They poured water in the radiator and waited for the overheated engine to cool.

By afternoon they were on Highway 99 in the valley. The truck's axle gave up as they drove through the cotton fields of Tulare. There was a clunk and then the truck lurched to a stop. Mother pulled up and got out. Daddy, already under the truck, called out,

"It's the axle; probably too much weight on one side."

"Can it be fixed?"

"The truck will have to be repacked."

"What about the axle?"

"Look for a straight branch that I can tie to connect the two sides of the axle. Maybe if we're lucky, that'll hold it together until we get to the town blacksmith."

Daddy could fix anything. He wrapped a cloth around the branch and the two broken ends of the axle, then reinforced it with wire. While Daddy improvised a repair, Mother went on into town to locate a blacksmith and then returned. The truck and Buick crawled into town like a funeral procession, and they held their breath until arriving at the blacksmith's.

As the cool night air came upon them, so did the mosquitoes. Soon a curtain of bugs swarmed around. Mother burned rags to keep them away while Daddy and the blacksmith gusseted the two pieces of the axle together. Hibbard and Marian retreated to the safety of the car, nursing bites that were on top of bites. Daddy repacked the truck so the weight was better balanced. They slept in the car and truck that night and started fresh in the morning.

By midday the family turned east. On the mountain roads, Marian silently watched Mother grip the steering wheel. It followed her every command. Before the car finished going to the left, the road turned to the right. Mother's eyes fixed on the road; her body stiffened at the start of each curve. She held her breath through it, breathed out, and let her body relax at the end of each and then stiffened again entering the next curve.

Looking out the window, Marian thought the mountains were beautiful, just as Daddy had promised. Thick trees surrounded the road. It looked like the mountains in "Heidi," the book

Marian was reading. She couldn't wait to get out of the car and go exploring. What treasures would she find? She didn't have to wait long.

A car passed Mother and she jerked to a stop.

"Get out," said Mother.

"What?"

"If I get in an accident, I don't want you to die, too."

"Die?"

"These roads are treacherous," and then almost to herself, "I don't know why I ever agreed to come up to these wretched mountains. Get out, Sis."

She opened the door and got out. She didn't know what else to do. Hibbard might have been able to make her laugh, or Daddy to calm her down, but Marian knew it was best to just do what Mother asked.

It was a steep hill and the air smelled so good. Daddy stopped and Hibbard jumped out to walk with Marian. It had been a long journey. Now in just a few more miles, they would explore their new home — just a few more miles. After being stuck in the car for hours, they were glad to be walking even for a few minutes. At the top of the hill, she got back into Mother's waiting car. The children rolled all the windows down so any little breeze could cool their sticky bodies.

They began seeing houses and cabins as they drove into West Point. Main Street was two blocks of dirt road. There was a bar, a school, a church, a store, and in a field next to Main Street, five tents were pitched in an encampment.

Mother shook her head and said, "Look! Those poor people have to live in tents. They can't possibly have any privacy."

"Why do they live in a tent?" asked Marian.

"They don't have anywhere else to live."

"Do they all share an outhouse?" asked Hibbard.

"I don't see an outhouse."

Marian saw a girl about her age. She recognized the fabric in the girl's dress. It was from a chicken-feed sack.* The girl's face was dirty and she had no shoes. Marian saw her watch the truck pass. Marian smiled at the girl, maybe she would be Marian's new friend. The girl stuck her tongue out at Marian and walked away. Marian slouched down in her seat, trying not to be seen.

They turned up another dirt road, Bald Mountain Road. They were almost home, their new home. Marian and Hibbard looked out one window and then the other trying to be the first to spot the cabin Daddy had described. Their luck was about to change. Daddy was a miner. It was just a matter of time before they were going to strike it rich! Everything was going to change now.

Daddy pulled the truck off the road and onto a driveway full of potholes. At the end was their cabin. Finally home! It was a small log cabin with the bark still on the logs. Curtains hung in the windows, and it looked just like Grandfather's cabin from Marian's book, "Heidi." She clapped her hands. They parked and all piled out. A burly man opened the cabin door and stepped out onto the porch; a woman with a baby on her hip followed.

Marian and Hibbard looked at each other, confused. Was this the wrong cabin? Had Daddy made a mistake? Was Marian's family going to share the cabin with another family? Mother had an expression of disbelief mixed with exhaustion. Daddy and the man started raising their voices at each other and Marian hid behind Hibbard thinking they might fight. Mother pulled on Daddy's arm, whispered something in his ear, and they turned and walked back to their cars. Daddy didn't try to hide his clenched fists.

Mother had tears in her eyes as she followed Daddy back to the encampment they had seen on their way into town. Mother waited in the car as Daddy bought a canvas tent at the store on Main Street. Mother and Marian started unpacking the car while Daddy and Hibbard set up the tent. The piano was the first thing Daddy unloaded from the truck. Mother looked at Daddy, disgusted, as he rolled it into the tent. Mother said not another word for the remainder of the night. Not to Daddy. Not to Hibbard. Not to Marian.

Angel

There are no secrets when you live in a tent.

All of Marian's family belongings were crammed between canvas walls. Marian's mother spent her days sweeping the dirt off the carpet that lay on the dirt inside the tent and cooking on an open flame outside. For Marian and Hibbard it was a surprise to be living in a tent after hearing stories about the cabin that Daddy had been promised. A family of four barely fit in the tent and their daily lives were lived out in full view of any passers-by.

Every morning Daddy left early to work the mine. When he returned at night, he and Mother barely spoke. Sometimes they pretended to talk to Marian but they were really talking to each other. Mother hardly looked at Daddy.

"Your daddy is full of promises. He's a dreamer. Always going to strike it rich."

"I am rich. Just look at your mother, children. See how rich I am? I am married to the prettiest woman in all of California."

The children smiled thinking Mother would smile too, but she shook her head and said, "As if living in a chicken coop wasn't bad enough, now we're in a tent. A tent!"

"There are other families who live in tents up here," said Marian.

Mother scowled, "We are not other families."

In the closest tent to Marian's family was a man who looked at the world with angry eyes. He scared Marian. He always looked ready to spring. Would he grab her or hit or yell? His wife looked exhausted and bothered by everything, including her hair that would not stay tied back. Her hands were for working, callused and flaking. Marian would have stayed away from their tent, but they had a two-year-old with soft curls. She had big brown eyes and cooed when she talked. She was too gentle for the roughness of the camp.

Marian's second night there, they heard the gruff voice of the child's father and the gritty mother's voice fill the encampment with shouting. Marian could hear thuds and then slaps. Pulling her blankets over her ears, she tried to block out the scary sounds from the neighboring tent. She fought back tears. Mother reached over and caressed her hair and Marian wondered if there was anyone to calm the little girl. Marian begged her mother to go and get her. Mother promised they would in the morning. She fell asleep crying, knowing the little girl was afraid. What awful sounds to sleep with, all alone.

With the first light, Marian was out of the tent. Mother was cooking pancakes and Daddy had already gone to his mine operation. Hibbard continued to sleep.

"Mother, can I check on the little girl?"

"Yes, but don't wake them. They were up late."

Marian ran to the neighboring tent. From inside came rustling sounds, then a shout.

"Get away from there!"

Marian jumped back.

"Don't touch that."

Marian heard a swat, followed by the little girl whimpering. Gulping, Marian stepped forward and asked, "Excuse me. Can the little girl come out and play."

The father snapped back the canvas flap, startling Marian. He stomped past her. The mother appeared in the opening trying to capture her loose hair and pin it down.

"What?"

"I, uh, we just got here a couple days ago."

"I know. We saw you drive in."

"I was wondering if your little girl wanted

to come over to play."

"Is it all right with your mother?"

"Yes."

"Don't let her get in your way. Send her back when you get tired of her."

The little girl peered around her mother.

Marian bent down, "Do you want to play?" The girl nodded and looked up at her mother who pushed her away. Marian held out her hand and the little girl took it. Marian led the little girl away.

The mother called after her, "You better behave yourself."

The little girl looked up at Marian but did not look back at her mother. Marian smiled down at her. When they got back to Marian's tent, Mother had already put a pancake on a plate for the girl and a pillow on the chair. Mother helped the girl up to the table and watched as she picked up the whole pancake with her fork, the watermelon syrup dripping off.

"Here, let me cut it for you," said Marian's mother. The girl withdrew her hand as if she had done something wrong. "It might be easier to eat."

The little girl stayed all day and followed Marian everywhere. Marian read stories to her, walked with her, carried her, fed her, laughed with her, combed her curly hair so gently it didn't hurt.

When her mother called her to come back to their own tent, the girl cried. But Marian wiped the little girl's eyes, calmed her, and promised to play again tomorrow.

The next day, the little girl was sitting outside Marian's tent in the dirt when Mother got up to cook Daddy's breakfast. Mother lifted the flap of the tent and in danced the little girl. She sat on the floor beside Marian watching her sleep. Marian opened her eyes to see the girl's smile. They giggled. Marian sat up and tickled the little girl. Laughter filled the tent. Mother set another place at the table outside and put a pillow on the chair for the little girl.

"What's their names?" asked the little girl.

"Who?"

"Your dolls."

"Oh, Patsyette and Baby Doll. What's your doll's name?"

"I don't have one."

"What do you mean? Oh, do you like to play with cars instead?"

"No."

"What do you play with?"

The little girl shrugged.

"Don't you have any toys?"

She shook her head.

Marian, Hibbard and Mother shared a glance.

"Do you want a doll?" Marian asked.

The little girl smiled but didn't say anything. Mother went in the tent and opened the trunk of fabric. The little girl held Baby Doll as Marian and Mother chose, cut, and sewed fabric. Hibbard spent the day carving a stool for the doll.

The little girl waited patiently and did not take her eyes off Marian and Marian's mother. When they finished, the little girl hugged her very own doll. The girl carried the doll around everywhere. Marian brought out the tea set and they had a doll's tea party. Before the little girl's mother called her back home, Marian read her a story.

The next day the girl was playing with her doll in the dirt outside Marian's tent again. Each morning Marian opened her eyes to an angel. Marian's family adored the little girl.

One morning Marian was not awakened by the little girl. Marian crawled out of her tent, and the neighbor's tent was gone.

"Gone. She's gone."

Marian ran to Mother who stood at the stove cooking twisters.

"Why? Where'd they go? "

Marian noticed Mother's eyes were moist, "I don't know."

Marian ran across the way and searched the ground where the tent had been. She looked for any clue of where they might have gone.

"It's like they were never here. Where did they go?"

"I don't know."

"When?"

"Sometime last night."

"I woke up last night. They were yelling."

"Yes."

"What was wrong?"

"I don't know."

"Another man yelled, too?"

"I think so."

"I thought I heard the other man yell, 'Thief'"

"Maybe."

"What were they saying?"

"I don't know. I wasn't listening."

"What did Daddy hear?"

"I didn't ask."

"Are they coming back?"

"I don't think so."

"What about the little girl? Is she going to

be all right?"

"She's such a sweet little girl."

"Oh, Mother...." Marian began to cry. Her mother caressed Marian's hair and hugged her tight. "I wish I had given her Baby Doll. Why didn't I give her Baby Doll?"

"You made her a doll that she loved."

"But it wasn't as good as Baby Doll."

"It was better than Baby Doll because you made it for her. She loved her doll."

"I wish I had known she was leaving. I wish I could have said goodbye."

Marian wiped her eyes, but the tears did not stop.

"I made twisters this morning," Mother said. "Come sit down."

Mother served her twisters as Marian looked over at the place where the tent once stood. Mother stood over her and squeezed Marian's shoulders looking at the empty place.

"Do you want watermelon syrup?" Mother asked.

Marian smiled up at her mother through the tears, "She loved Daddy's watermelon syrup."

"Yes, she did."

Making a Splash

Marian and Hibbard begged Mother to go to the swimming hole where all the children played on the Middle Fork of the Mokelumne River. She cautioned about falling in mine shafts, and the children said they would be careful. She worried about rattlesnakes.

"We'll keep an eye open for them," said Marian.

"By the time you see them, it will be too late. Carry some potassium permanganate* in case you get bit," said Mother.

"All right," said Hibbard.

Finally, Mother decided she would pack a picnic lunch and go along. The children ran and skipped down the trail toward the swimming hole. They knew they were getting close when the air filled with the sounds of splashing and children's voices. A dozen children were playing, swimming, swinging on a rope, splashing, and letting the stream of a waterfall run over their bodies.

Mother wore a lacy, flowered dress and flower-rimmed, straw hat. She sat on the bank of the river near Mrs. Sparling and her three boys, Jodean, who was the same age as Hibbard, Jerry, who was the same age as Marian, and John, who was a couple years younger. Usually when Mother talked to people from West Point, she had a stiffness in her body, as if she felt she must show her upbringing, but when she talked with Mrs. Sparling, they sat together like old friends. The conversation flowed easily, and Mother even laughed. The Sparlings were outsiders, too, arriving a few months earlier. The two families instantly became friends.

The children went to the water's edge and stepped in. All around Hibbard the water turned purple. Hibbard looked down and shook his head realizing why. Jodean asked, and Hibbard whispered, "My mother is worried we might get bit by a rattlesnake. She almost didn't let us come. Finally, she said we could if I carried treatment in my pocket. So now I'm a potassium permanganate tea bag."

They laughed and dove in the water. Marian inched her way to the waterfall and felt a steady stream over her head and back. She was mesmerized watching children swinging out on a rope and splashing into the deepest part of the river.

"Brubby, that looks so fun. Do you think I could do it?"

"Sure, Sis. The children are standing in line over there," he said, pointing to a boulder on the bank of the river.

She got out of the water and ran into line. Each child took a turn and then it was Marian's. She let the girl behind go in front of her. Marian searched the girl for a trace of fear, but the girl grabbed onto the rope, yelled, "Watch out below!" and splashed into the river. The children behind Marian pushed forward. Marian stepped up to the rope, gripped it, and swung out over the deepest part of the river. She screamed and held on: she didn't let go. Marian swung back, her feet scraping the safety of the boulder. All the children in line, sighed a collective, "Ah, Come on."

More than anything Marian wanted to be like that girl, sheer joy instead of panic. But Marian looked down at the river as if it were muck from a hog ranch. Oh how she wished she had learned to swim at the Plunge last summer. She tried but she was, without a doubt, the worst swimming student of 1934. Water got in her nose. She swam into other people and the wall. She wouldn't open her eyes underwater, and she couldn't coordinate her breathing with the rotation of her arms. Standing on the boulder holding onto the rope, she remembered her swimming teacher consoling her, "Don't feel bad, Marian. Some people are just boards in the water. You aren't meant to swim." Marian begged her mother not to go back. But Mother, having been a teacher, never gave up on a student and insisted Marian learn. The next week Marian returned to the Plunge, and her swimming teacher just shook her head and clicked her tongue saying, "Your mother's wasting her money." At the end of seven weeks, Marian still sunk when she tried to float, got water in her nose, and was out of sync with her breathing. If she had learned to swim at the Plunge in Fontana, her toes wouldn't be bunched up underneath her, trying to crawl backwards.

A big boy behind Marian, Rodney, called out, "She's a chicken."

His younger sister and brother began to, "Bwack! Bwack!" All three flapped their elbows like chicken wings.

Hibbard swam clumsily to the center of the river and called up to Marian, "You can do it, Sis. I'm here. I'd never let anything bad happen to you."

Rodney's brother and sister continued chanting, "Chicken! Chicken!"

Marian looked back at them and then down to her brother. Now there was Hibbard's new friend, Jodean, with him moving his arms, so he could stay afloat.

"Leave her alone," yelled Jodean.

Jerry and John, Jodean's brothers, swam out too, "It's fun," yelled John.

"You're going to love it," said Jerry.

"Don't worry. We'll get you back to the shallow end," said Hibbard.

Marian looked out at her best friend, Hibbard, and her three new friends. She smiled at them, closed her eyes, took a breath. She backed up, clinging to the rope, and ran. She leapt off the edge of the boulder with eyes closed, screaming louder than anyone else.

Hibbard and the boys yelled, "Let Go! Let Go!"

Marian let go and splashed into the water.

The boys quickly surrounded her, and Hibbard reached into the water to pull Marian up. She opened her eyes and laughed, "That's so fun!" The boys laughed and swam her to shore. Rodney splashed in like a cannon ball, drenching everyone.

When Marian stepped out of the water, she said, "Brubby, let's do that again."

"I'll wait for you in the water," said Hibbard.

Marian ran back into line and waited with a chilled excitement. Mother looked up and called to Hibbard, "Is Sis all right?"

"She's great," said Hibbard.

"Watch out for her."

"I am, Mother."

Hibbard waited in the water to help his sister to the shore. At first, he waited for her right where she splashed in, and then he backed up a little and then a little more until she swung, splashed, and swam the dog paddle with such confidence that Hibbard watched his sister from the shore and finally, proudly from his spot in line.

As the afternoon shadows lengthened, children began to leave the swimming hole. Mother and Mrs. Sparling announced to their children that it was time to go home. The children packed up and chased each other down the path. When they got to the road, Marian's family and the Sparlings each went different directions. Mother bubbling with news, practically danced back to the tent.

"Mrs. Sparling thought there might be a cabin available for a nice family up Bald Mountain Road," said Mother.

"So we can move out of the tent?" asked Hibbard.

"Yes! Reverend Kirk's mother-in-law is moving with her son, John, to Southern California for seminary. They want someone to live in their cabin so squatters don't move in."

"Mrs. Kunkle's cabin?" asked Marian.

"Yes, if they haven't given it to someone else. Daddy and I will talk with Reverend Kirk and Penninah, first thing tomorrow."

"You never would have met Mrs. Sparling if we hadn't gone to the river today," said Hibbard.

"Yes, I suppose you're right," said Mother.

"And if you didn't meet Mrs. Sparling you wouldn't have known about Mrs. Kunkle's cabin."

"I suppose not."

"It's good we went to the river, today. Isn't it?"

Mother tried to hide her smile and said, "Yes, I suppose."

The next day the family put on their best clothes and walked over to the church on Main Street. Marian's parents talked to the Reverend and his wife. It was a one-room cabin but Daddy had carpenter skills. He could build bunk beds on the back porch for the children and he would rig up a canvas wall that could be raised in the warm weather and lowered when it rained or snowed. Daddy promised to build on a separate kitchen.

When Reverend Kirk said, "Well it sounds like it is all settled then," Mother burst into tears.

"An answer to my prayers," said Mother. "I

was so worried that we would still be in the tent when it started to snow."

Watermelon Seeds

Mother balanced the blackberry pie in one hand and smoothed the frilly skirt of her cotton dress with the other. She straightened her flower-rimmed straw hat. Marian stood on one foot and wiped road dust from the toe of her Girl Scout oxfords on the back of her calf and then shifted her weight and wiped the other. She realized she would need to crumple up more newspaper to stuff in the toe when she got home because the shoes were loose again. Mother looked down at Marian, took off her white glove, and moistened her thumb to wipe the corner of Marian's mouth. Marian cringed, hoping that the children inside had not seen. She could hear their voices. She fingered the red and white plaid skirt of the dress Barbara Dell had given her the day she left Fontana. Marian wished Barbara Dell were there, and she hoped she would make new friends here. The voices spilling out the cracks of the wall of the cabin piqued Marian's curiosity.

"Patoo!" "Patoo!" "Patoo!" "Patoo!"

"Hey! I just got another one in!!!"

"That's only cuz you're sittin' closer."

"Is not."

"If I were sittin' where you're sittin' I'd get 'um in too."

"Na uh! It's my aim!"

"More like your luck."

"It's aim. Ya' gotta use your tongue."

"Ya' don't know nothin'."

"I got two in. I must know somethin'."

"That's cuz you're sittin' closer!"

"Two to what...? What? Oh, nothin'?"

Mother and Marian heard a loud thump and then footsteps running. Then a thud and a woman screamed, "You two knock it off." Mother and daughter stood on the doorstep listening, not sure if they should back away from the house or knock. The footsteps slowed, a chair scraped across the floor and then it grew quiet again except for "Patoo!"

Mother took a breath and then knocked. A large dog attacked the door from the other side; Marian jumped off the step. And the woman hollered, "Lie down!" They heard footsteps, a swat, a dog whimper, and then the door swung open.

Mrs. Porter was short, plump and wore a misbuttoned cotton dress with no shoes. She held a one-year-old boy with a grimy T-shirt on her hip. A toddler, clinging to her mother's dress, stared up at Marian through her tangled hair. Marian

smiled at her, but the girl ran to her sister and brothers who were seated on the bench of a long plank table.

Mother handed Mrs. Porter the pie she had baked and introduced herself. Mrs. Porter invited them in. Mother stepped in and over a doll on the floor as if it were not even there. Marian followed her. Marian's eyes adjusted to the light of the cabin lit by a single lantern and light sneaking in through the cracks in the walls. She saw a cup under the table and clothes draped over the end of the bench. Mrs. Porter hurried to a seat, scooped up papers and toys and took them out of sight, then quickly returned wiping the chair with her hand. Standing by the stove was a teenage girl stirring a large pot of beans. Sitting at the table was a boy about Hibbard's age, a girl about Marian's age, another boy a little younger and the two-year-old girl who had come to the door. Everyone stopped and stared as Mother and Marian came in and sat down in the chairs that Mrs. Porter had just emptied out. Mother explained they had been at church and that Reverend Kirk had told Mother about their family because the children were about the same age. Rodney, the boy who was about Hibbard's age, stared Marian in the eye and then turned back to spitting seeds.

"Patoo."

The other children turned away, ignoring them. Each had a chunk of watermelon in their hands, juice dripping between their fingers.

"Patoo."

Only then did Marian see all over the floor were watermelon seeds. The three children were aiming for the holes and cracks in the floor. Did their mother know they were spitting — spitting inside the house? Mother and Mrs. Porter continued talking about Reverend Kirk's church and Sunday school. Marian turned back when she heard the younger boy yell, "Rebecca, get out of the way."

Irma laughed, "Yeah, You're gonna get hit by a flying seed."

The little girl squealed as she ran out of reach of her older brothers and sister. She turned and spat on the floor. Rodney and Wayne grabbed each other and exploded with laughter. Irma ran over and scooped up her little sister, swung her around and plopped her on the bench. Rebecca giggled, looked up at Wayne and spat at him.

"Hey!" yelled Wayne, as he wiped his shirt and pushed her away from him. Rebecca screeched.

Rodney punched Wayne, "Leave her alone."

"She spitted at me," Wayne whined.

Irma moved Rebecca to her lap and hugged

her, "She don't know any better."

Rebecca squirmed out of Irma's lap and ran to her mother wailing. The baby woke up and began crying.

Marian's mother stood up and said, "Well, I guess it's time for us to go." Marian quickly stood and followed her mother to the door. Mrs. Porter thanked Mother for the pie, and they made promises that they would visit each other again. But Marian knew they never would.

Mother and Marian walked silently for about a half a mile. Mother sighed and shook her head. And then Marian started to say, "Mother, they were — "

"I know, Marian. They just don't know any better."

Defending Family

"Take it back!!" Hibbard yelled.

"And your mother wears those frilly dresses and gloves, thinking she's better than the rest of the world," said Rodney.

"She does not."

"Your dad is nothing but a gopher, crawling underground. You're nothing but a dressed-up gopher family. My sis gets a nickel for every gopher she catches. Feeds 'em to the dogs. Gonna tell her to stop on by."

"Take it back!"

"Make me!"

Hibbard lunged at Rodney and down they went. Fists flew as they rolled through the stinky groundcover, each struggling to get control.

Marian watched her brother in horror. Hibbard never fought. Rodney fought for what he wanted, fought to keep what he had, and fought for the sheer fun of it. Rodney had a fighter's body, big and bulky, while Hibbard's delicate body often gave in to wheezing when asthma attacked. But Hibbard was fighting Rodney.

This was not the first time Rodney had teased them. Rodney's grandfather had sold the

Ferguson mine to a local miner who sold it to another miner who sold it to a businessman from Santa Monica who was a friend of Grandpa's and sold it to Daddy. According to Rodney, there was no more gold in the mine.

"Your dad's a fool. He wasted his money. My granddad got all the gold."

Marian's family knew differently. Daddy told them he found gold — not a lot yet, but some. And when Daddy didn't find gold one day, he stayed in the mine longer the next. Marian knew if Rodney's family didn't find any more gold, they hadn't worked hard enough. She didn't think about the times when they couldn't get what was on their shopping list because they ran out of money. Marian couldn't let doubt creep in. She just knew her daddy was right.

Rodney, on top of Hibbard, was clobbering him. Marian jumped on Rodney's back and tried to push him over. She wasn't strong enough. Rodney didn't budge. Marian heard Reverend Kirk hollering from his house across the street, but she kept right on pushing and hitting.

"Get off my brother, you moose!"

Reverend Kirk ran over and peeled Marian off Rodney, then pulled Rodney to his feet. "Stop this right now!"

Marian shoved a finger in Rodney's face, "He started it!"

"Your crazy brother attacked me!" Rodney said, swatting at Marian's hand and wiping blood from his nose.

Reverend Kirk stepped in between them. "That's enough. All of you, get on the bus."

Marian helped Hibbard up, but he pulled away from her and limped to the bus. His back was covered with dirt and sprigs of the brush they'd rolled through. His torn sleeve hung by threads.

The children piled into the converted Cadillac that served as their school bus. Reverend Kirk worked at the community church next door to the school. He had welded the "bus" together from several cars, a Cadillac front and back with an extra car body welded in the middle so ten children could ride that bus to school. The drive to school, usually full of chatting and laughing, was quiet except for whispers, accompanied by quick glances from the other children. Marian sat next to Hibbard and brought her handkerchief up to wipe the blood from his eyebrow, but he pushed away her hand, crossed his arms and stared hard out the window.

When Reverend Kirk pulled up to school, he marched Hibbard and Rodney in to Mr. Davis, who was not only Hibbard and Rodney's teacher but also in charge of the school. At recess, Hibbard did not come out to the playground.

Marian asked Mr. Davis, "What happened to my brother?"

"What do you think happens to boys who fight?"

She didn't know. Hibbard had never fought before. At lunch Marian couldn't find Hibbard. By the end of the day, Marian was crazy with worry. Marian rushed out of her classroom, but Hibbard did not come to the bus. Fighting back tears, she asked Reverend Kirk what happened to Hibbard.

"Your father had to pick him up."

The bus was a capsule of laughter and chattering. Marian sat silently staring out of the window. She wondered why Daddy hadn't picked her up. She was fighting too. She knew the school sent Hibbard home as punishment, but Marian wondered if it was. She couldn't imagine that he got in trouble at home, not after Daddy and Mother heard what Rodney had said. Marian wished they were back in Fontana where they had friends.

When Marian got home, she slipped out to their sleeping porch and found Hibbard curled up in his bunk reading. Marian climbed up on the lower bunk and peered over the railing of the top bunk at her brother.

"I was so scared. What happened?"

"Got suspended," he said without looking up.

"What did Daddy do?"

"He dropped me off saying he'd talk to me later."

"Where is he?"

"Back at the mine."

"Did you tell him what Rodney said?"

"To Pop, but not Mom."

"Are you hurt?"

"Nah."

"I'm glad you hit him."

Although Marian didn't see it, she thought Hibbard smiled. Marian jumped off the bunk and walked back into the cabin. Mother looked up from mending Hibbard's shirt. The shirt smelled like the plant at the bus stop where they fought. Marian's stomach instantly became queasy.

"I'm disappointed with both of you."

"But Rodney started it. He really did. He's always so mean. Not just to us. To everybody. Brubby had to stop him."

"Rodney doesn't know any better. You two do. I expect better from you."

Marian wanted to convince Mother that

Rodney really did deserve it but she knew there was no point. So she said, "Sorry," and changed the subject. She reached across the table and found a sprig of the ground covering in the seam of Hibbard's shirt.

"What's this plant? It's so stinky."

"I'm not sure. Let's look it up."

Marian got out the book that they used to look up plants that grew from Fontana to the Sierra. She searched the pages comparing the sprig with the pictures in the book. She finally found it under the "M's."

Marian smiled, "Is this it?"

"Yep, it sure looks like it."

"Mountain Misery. That's a perfect name."

First Snow

"Brubby, wake up! There's snow on the floor!"

"Snow?"

"Yeah, look, it's on the floor against the wall."

The children threw back their covers, jumped out of bed. Hibbard pulled up the canvas that covered the opening in the wall of their sleeping porch. Marian's big toe smooshed snow on the floor as she looked out at the black branches outlined with a white powder.

"It's beautiful," said Hibbard.

"It looks magical, just like looking out Heidi's grandfather's window. Mother! Daddy! It snowed last night!"

Mother threw open the door of the sleeping porch, "Quick, come warm yourself by the fire."

The children ran barefoot into the house to get close to the wood-burning stove.

"Can we play outside?"

"Not in your pajamas."

"If we get dressed?"

"I suppose. But not long. It's a school day."

The children practically knocked each other

over trying to get into the sleeping porch to grab their clothes, then back to the wood-burning stove to get dressed. Marian put on a skirt, two shirts and her longest knee highs. She adjusted the cardboard in her shoe so it was centered over the hole in the sole. Then they barreled out the front door.

"Careful of the ice," Daddy called as Hibbard slipped on the front steps. Marian stopped and tiptoed down the stairs.

Grabbing a handful of snow, Marian immediately hurled it in the direction of Hibbard but he, even quicker, had already launched his snowball at her. Marian laughed, brushing the snow off her skirt, and leapt out of sight behind the closest tree. They peeked out, quickly pulled back again and then crept to better hiding places. Snowball after snowball flew before Mother called them in for breakfast. It was hard to obey, but after one more snowball, the children came in. They ate oatmeal and then changed clothes for school. All their clothes were for Southern California weather, so Marian put on two dresses, the red plaid over another cotton one, her knee highs, her light coat, and hat. She put a new piece of cardboard in her shoes and handed a piece to Hibbard. They had no mittens or scarves, but

Marian put up her collar and her hands in her pockets as she left.

The walk to school was filled with ducking and taking cover as snowballs hurled through the air. First, it was just Marian and Hibbard, but when they passed the Sparling place, the boys ran down their driveway to join the snowball fight. They were dressed in boots, warm coats, mittens, scarves and hats that covered their ears. Down the road a little ways, the Porter children laid in wait hiding out of sight — Irma behind a log about a hundred feet from Rodney and Wayne across the road between them. Marian heard Rodney whistle and Irma whistle back. Marian spun around but too late. The three Porter children leapt out and ambushed them. Snowballs were coming from all sides. The Porters had lived through many seasons of snow in West Point. They were expert snowball fighters. There was no defense except to run. The Porter children wore clothes that had survived many snows and had been passed from one child to the next as each grew. Some stretched to cover the body and other pieces hung loosely. All had frayed edges and were covered with grime and holes.

Marian didn't feel the cold until she got to Bummersville Station where Reverend Kirk picked up the children and took them the rest of the way to school. When she sat on the bus, her knees were the same color as her red plaid dress. Her feet were soaked and snow melted on her shoulders. Marian's fingers were bright red. She blew on them to thaw them out and then rubbed her knees. She shivered with delight.

Christmas in the Mountains

A couple Sundays before Christmas, Penninah Kirk and another woman from church, dressed in their Sunday best, arrived unannounced at the cabin. They carried an overflowing basket of food. Marian opened the door and was excited they had come to visit. She loved Mrs. Kirk.

"We thought you could use a little help this Christmas," said Mrs. Kirk as she handed Marian the basket.

Hibbard rushed over to help Marian, but Daddy pushed his chair away from the table and called to the women, "We don't need charity. We're just fine."

"But Daddy, there's chocolate."

"Marian! Get in here!"

Mother shook her head, "They don't mean any harm."

Daddy jumped up, furious, and stood in the doorway. Nothing was going to cross that threshold, in or out.

Daddy smiled at Mrs. Kirk, "Penninah, I'm sure there are other people who need your charity. We don't."

Then Daddy closed the door; he didn't

exactly slam it — but close to it. Marian was horrified; Daddy had closed the door on Mrs. Kirk when she was just being nice. Didn't he remember Mrs. Kirk was the pastor's wife? Didn't he remember that Mrs. Kirk's mother, Mrs. Kunkle, was letting them stay in her cabin while she was gone? How could Daddy be so mean? As soon as the door shut, Mother started crying and Daddy started shouting. Marian and Hibbard escaped to their sleeping porch.

Once a month the family drove forty-five minutes to Jackson to buy food and the supplies they needed. The children always looked forward to their monthly shopping trip, leaving early in the morning and not returning until evening. On the way home, they stopped in Mokelumne Hill, and Marian and Hibbard got a Nesbitt orange soda for a nickel. This December Daddy kept delaying the shopping trip hoping he would find a rich vein of ore. Finally, on the day before Christmas Eve, Mother put her foot down and insisted that they go.

"Tomorrow we have to go. We are out of flour," said Mother. "Marian and I have baking to do."

Marian was relieved. She thought they

wouldn't have Christmas at all this year. They had no tree. No decorations. No ornaments. Santa probably didn't even know where they had moved. At least they would have their traditional jam cookies.

That night as they lay in their bunk beds, Hibbard said, "We have to stay home tomorrow."

"Why?"

"To make our gift for Mother and Pop."

"If we stay home, we won't get an orange soda."

"We can get one next month."

"All right, what are we going to make?"

"I found a picture in my book. I'll show you tomorrow."

The next morning, Mother and Daddy drove off as the children waved goodbye. As soon as they were out of sight, the children ran inside. Hibbard pulled the book off the shelf and showed Marian a picture of squirrel bookends.

"Wow! Can we really make those?"

"Yep."

Hibbard ran out back and got some scrap wood he had hidden. He drew the squirrels on the wood and cut them out with Daddy's saw. As Hibbard cut the rest of the wood, Marian sanded the edges of the squirrels until they were smooth.

All morning they were in the back of their cabin drawing, sawing, and sanding.

"I wish we had some paint," said Marian.

"I saw some grey paint on the front porch. It's the same color grey as the window frames."

"Where is it?"

"At the end of the porch."

"I'll get it."

Marian ran to the front of the house.

"Brubby. Come quick! Look."

Hibbard ran to the front, "Where did that come from?"

"I don't know. It was here when I came around the corner."

"Is there a note on it?"

"No."

"Who would do that?"

Marian shrugged. She looked around to see if she could see anyone hiding. "Do you think Daddy will let us keep it?"

"He can't make us give it back. It's already cut."

"But he won't take charity."

"It's not charity; it's a Christmas tree."

"He's going to make us give it back just like he made us give the basket of food back."

"But we knew the church ladies brought the

basket. We don't know who brought us the tree."

"So, you think he'll let us keep it?"

"Maybe. Let's take it in. We could decorate the tree before Daddy gets home."

Hibbard made a stand for it and Marian collected pine cones. Together they carried it into the cabin and put it in the corner away from the wood-burning stove. Marian skipped to the back of the cabin with the grey paint, and the two of them painted all the parts of the bookends. When they were dry, Hibbard nailed the pieces together and Marian wrapped newspaper around the gift, tied it with twine, and put it under the tree.

The children tried to stay up until their parents got home but it got too late so they made themselves bean sandwiches and went to bed. Sometime in the middle of the night, Marian thought she heard the sound of sleigh bells and footsteps on the roof of their sleeping porch. She sat up but hearing nothing more, she knew she was dreaming. It was foolish to think Santa would know where they were.

The next morning freezing temperatures woke them. Snow was on the floor of their sleeping porch.

Hibbard whispered, "Marian, are you awake?"

"Um hmm. I think it snowed last night."

"Yeah. It did. Merry Christmas."

"Merry Christmas."

"Come on."

They threw back their covers and ran barefoot into the cabin to warm up by the stove. The cabin smelled like cinnamon. Mother was baking. Daddy was sitting at the table reading. The children ran and hugged them.

"Merry Christmas, Mother. Merry Christmas, Daddy. Did you see the Christmas tree?"

"Yes, it is beautiful."

Hibbard gasped, "Marian, look!"

The tree was covered in shimmering tinsel, and hanging in the middle of the tree were two pairs of mittens. A large pair of blue ones and a smaller red pair.

"Santa found us! Mother, Santa found us! I heard his sleigh bells on the roof last night. It was him. I thought I was dreaming. He was on our roof last night."

Marian put on the red mittens. They were so soft and warm. She wore them all day except when she ate, and only took them off then because her mother insisted.

The Blue Buick

Two men pulled up in front of the cabin. At first Marian was excited, thinking they had visitors. But nobody ever visited. When the men got out of the car they scowled. Marian didn't know if they were tired or mad or hurt or a little of all three. The older one chewed on a cigar; he wore a fedora like Daddy's and an old suit that had seen better days. He was clearly in charge. The younger one chewed on a matchstick. He wore a corduroy coat with a bluejean shirt and black felt hat. His pants were held up by a rope belt. His callused hands had scabs on the knuckles. When they walked to the cabin, the older looked like he owned the place while the younger looked around to make sure no one was going to sneak up on them from behind. Marian and Hibbard peered down on them from a pine tree.

The one in charge nodded his head toward the side of the house and said, "There it is."

"There what is?" whispered Marian.

The other man looked around.

"Shush," whispered Hibbard.

Thinking they were alone, the older one almost seemed sad as he said, "I hope he doesn't give us any trouble."

The other one just smiled.

They knocked on the door so hard it shook the hinges. Mother opened the door, wiping her hands on her apron.

The man took off his fedora and said, "We're looking for your husband, Ma'am."

"He's in the mine, working. What's this about?"

"Is that your Buick, Ma'am?"

"Yes," Mother said through clenched teeth.

"Well, you see Ma'am..." the older man's voice was muffled as he took out paperwork from inside his breast pocket and the other man shuffled his feet. Mother covered her mouth, closed her eyes as if to momentarily shut out what the man said and shook her head. The children knew the news the men brought was not good. They strained to hear. Mother called to Hibbard.

"Go get your Daddy."

Hibbard climbed out of the tree and ran to the mine. Mother continued talking to the older man on the porch and Marian climbed down slowly and inched closer. Daddy ran up wiping dirt from his clothes and hands before extending his hand to shake.

The man got right to the point, "We've come

to pick up the car."

"I just need a little more time."

"My boss has waited five months."

Daddy raised his voice, "I just need a little more time. When I get this ore to the smelter, I'll have the money."

"Boss is tired of waiting."

The younger man unbuttoned his coat and threatened, "You don't want to do it this way." Marian saw a gun tucked in his waistband.

"Marian, Hibbard, get inside," Mother snapped.

Marian heard Daddy curse, and Mother plead as she closed the door. Hibbard and Marian stood inside not sure what to do. They paced the floor as the men yelled at each other outside. The door opened, and Mother came in fighting back tears. She started kneading the bread dough she had left on the table. Her back was to the children, but her shoulders were quivering. Marian took a step toward her when she heard a car engine start and then a second. Mother punched the bread dough. Marian stopped and looked at Hibbard.

The door was thrown open, and Daddy stormed in. Marian jumped out of his way. He grabbed his coffee cup off the counter, and coffee splashed on him. He plucked up a dish towel, wiped himself and the floor, and threw it back on the counter. He tossed the remaining coffee into the sink, grabbed the percolator, singed his hand, dropped it, snatched the dish towel to pick up the percolator and poured himself a cup of hot coffee. Then he slammed the percolator back on the stove, threw the dish towel on the counter, and sank down into the couch.

Mother had her back to Daddy and whimpered. She shaped the loaves and put them on the stove to rise. She kept her back to him, picked up the towel, folded it, and put it down again.

Marian looked at Daddy and then Mother, and when she caught Hibbard's eye, they sneaked out. They looked at the empty spot where the Buick had been parked. Then they walked silently for a long time. Hibbard kicked a small rock and Marian kicked it and then Hibbard did. They traded it back and forth until it landed out of sight and they started with a new rock.

"How are we going to live out here without a car?" asked Marian.

"Don't know. Daddy will have to figure out something," said Hibbard.

"I wish we had never moved up here."

Marian kicked another rock, and it landed

right by an opening of a large hole in the ground.

"Hey, look, an old mine hole," said Hibbard.

"Can you see the bottom?"

"No, it's too dark."

"I wonder how deep it is?"

"Let's throw a rock down."

The children lay on their bellies and tossed rocks into the mining hole listening how long the rock fell until it hit the bottom of the hole.

"Has it hit bottom yet?"

"No, not yet."

"How much longer do you think?"

"Shush."

Marian whispered, "It's a long way down."

Appendicitis

Hibbard tiptoed out of the sleeping porch into the main room of the cabin.

"Mother, Sis is worse."

She threw back her covers and ran to the bunk bed.

"Marian?"

Marian moaned.

Hibbard came with a lit kerosene lantern. Marian was rolled into a ball, pulling her knees up into her stomach.

"Marian, where does it hurt?"

She moaned.

"Can you point to where it hurts."

She stretched her legs out as far as she could and pushed up her stomach.

"All over," she said pointing to her right side. "I feel like I'm going to get sick."

Mother picked up the pot that Marian had gone to bed with and set it down next to her, "How long have you been awake?"

"Haven't been to sleep yet," Marian said, shaking.

Then the pain silenced Marian's voice.

Mother sat on Marian's bed and cradled her

while Hibbard's eyes desperately asked Mother what he should do. Mother looked at Hibbard blankly. She had no idea.

"Hibbard, what are we going to do? Marian needs to get to the doctor. The nearest one is forty minutes away by car. We don't have the Buick anymore."

"But Pop went to get a car in Stockton."

"He was going to try. We don't know if he's going to have any luck, and we can't wait for him any longer. Marian needs to get to the doctor tonight."

"Tonight?"

"Hibbard, this is serious. She might not make it through the night."

"What about Reverend Cole? When Daddy left, the Reverend said to let him know if we needed anything."

"Reverend Cole! That's it. Run to his house and tell him Betty Jane needs to get to the doctor."

Hibbard was grabbing his shoes but stopped to look back at his Mother when she called Marian by the wrong name. Betty Jane was their older sister. The children knew she died when she was a baby a long time ago in New Mexico. She got the measles from some other children and when it developed into pneumonia she died. Mother never got over it: she never talked about it. But anytime Hibbard or Marian were sick or injured Mother frantically applied a mustard plaster or Vicks VapoRub, fixed onion gargle, boiled grapefruit skins or chamomile tea. When they went to play in the woods, Mother insisted Hibbard always carry potassium permanganate in a handkerchief in his pocket to use in case they got bit by a snake. Mother was always ready with a remedy.

"Hibbard, help me move Marian to my bed in the front room by the stove." They tucked her in. "Now mind. Hurry, Hibbard. Be sure to tell Reverend Cole how urgent it is."

Hibbard ran the two miles to Reverend Cole's.

Mother started a fire in the wood-burning stove. She caressed Marian's hair and arms. Then Mother remembered the pot from the sleeping porch; she retrieved it and tucked it next to Marian. She took the encyclopedia off the shelf, opened it up on the table and flipped through the pages to find appendix. She leaned over the book reading. It explained what an appendix looked like, its purpose, symptoms of acute appendicitis attack, but under the heading of care/what to do, it said to seek medical attention immediately. The book warned that left unattended it could rupture,

releasing toxins throughout the body and ultimately result in death. Mother pushed the book across the table in horror.

Marian vomited. Fortunately, Mother had no time to dwell on what she had read. She gently washed Marian, dressed her in clean clothes and packed another change. Just then, Reverend Cole and Hibbard ran in and carried Marian in Mother's blankets to the back seat of his old black Model T. Mother was already in the front seat when she remembered something and ran back into the cabin, returning a moment later with a piece of paper that she put in her purse. She kissed Hibbard's forehead and said, "Hibbard, now mind. You're going to need to stay and watch over the place. When Daddy comes home, tell him what happened."

Reverend Cole drove forty minutes to Sutter Creek, late at night down bumpy dirt roads. Mother woke the doctor. The reverend carried Marian in. The doctor prodded, poked and pushed on her stomach as Marian winced and screeched. He hit the heel of Marian's foot and she grabbed her stomach in pain.

"Uh huh, just as I thought. She needs to get to the hospital, tonight. It's her appendix. Close to rupturing."

Reverend Cole was already scooping up Marian. "Where's the hospital?"

"Sacramento."

"But Sacramento is over an hour away."

"That's the closest one."

Mother burst into tears.

"I wish there was something more I could do for her," said the doctor.

"Don't worry, Mrs. Moore," said Reverend Cole. "We'll get her there in time."

The doctor patted Mother's shoulder as he rushed past to open the office and car doors for Reverend Cole who laid Marian back in the car bed. Then he handed her a little card to hold with a picture of Jesus on it. She looked out the window and saw the doctor shaking his head as he looked at his pocket watch; then he turned out the light and Marian saw the black sky with little dots of light. She felt Mother's caress. The intense pain felt like she was being eaten from the inside out.

Reverend Cole drove, and Mother recounted the week through her tears, "It started as a tummy ache. I made her chamomile tea and when the pain continued, I prayed but I thought she had gas or she ate something that didn't agree with her or she had the stomach flu. But the pain persisted, each day getting worse." Then Mother told about Betty Jane catching the measles and pneumonia. "She went from a hospital bed to a coffin." She talked about losing their farm in Fontana. "We dreamed that mining gold was the answer. My husband had studied to be a mining engineer. I thought our luck was going to shift, but it has turned out worse than it was in Fontana. And since our car was taken we have been so isolated. The cabin's too far out of town. And my husband left two days before Marian got sick. When I needed him most, he was gone. But it all started as a tummy ache. It was just a tummy ache."

Arriving at the hospital, Reverend Cole left the car running as he carried Marian up the grand staircase. A matron stepped in front of him. "You've got to pay to be seen by a doctor here," she said. "This isn't a charity hospital."

"My daughter is very sick. A doctor in Sutter Creek said she needed surgery tonight."

"Surgeries cost a lot of money. How will you pay?"

Mother reached in her purse and pulled out a check she had received that week from the government. It was the Great War veterans bonus check. Four hundred dollars had been issued to Daddy. Mother waved the check and said, "I have money."

The matron snatched the check and pointed down the corridor. Reverend Cole laid Marian on a gurney and nurses rolled her into a brightly lit room. There were three nurses and two doctors each covered in white coats, gloves, masks, and caps. Marian could only see their eyes.

"I'm giving you ether," said one of the nurses. "It'll help you relax. This mask goes over your mouth and nose. Just breathe normally."

Marian's body felt like tiny little pieces floating up toward the ceiling. She saw the three nurses and two doctors she had seen earlier, but she also saw another man standing in the room, behind the doctors and nurses. It was the man in the picture that Reverend Cole gave her. He did not wear a mask or coat or gloves. He stood there watching over her and the operation. She was no longer in pain, no longer afraid and then, no longer awake.

When Marian came out of surgery, Reverend Cole drove back to West Point but Mother stayed by Marian's side, sleeping in the chair next to the bed. Over the next week, the nurses kept meticulous records of everything that Marian ate and what she didn't. Even though Mother was hungry, she wouldn't eat any of the food that

Marian couldn't finish. Her meals included orange sherbet, quite a treat. One day when it was 105 degrees, Mother was clearly uncomfortably hot. Marian gave Mother the orange sherbet to eat, but Mother refused, and the nurse took away the tray with the orange sherbet that they both wanted.

On the third night in the hospital, Marian awoke to the sound of her Daddy's voice. She thought she was dreaming, but when she opened her eyes, there he was, standing right at her bedside looking down at her. He brought her a present — red silk pajamas with golden dragons embroidered down the front. He drove through the night to make sure Marian was all right and then he returned to Hibbard in West Point.

At the end of the week when Marian was released from the hospital, Mother decided to take her to Sutter Creek where a woman took care of sick people in her home. With a ruptured appendix, Marian needed additional care for at least a couple of weeks. Daddy and Hibbard drove them to Sutter Creek. They made a bed in the back of the truck, and Hibbard watched over Marian as Daddy drove slowly over bumps and around curves. Hibbard told her all the news, "Mrs. Kunkle came back."

"Are we going to have to live in the tent again?"

"No, but Daddy couldn't find anything in West Point. Reverend Kirk knew about a place in Glencoe, behind the home of a widow, Mrs. Curnow. She came from the gold mines of South Africa. Daddy and I packed up all our belongings and Reverend Kirk helped us move. And our new school is right down the road, within walking distance and you'll never guess the name of it — Mosquito Gulch School."

Marian started to laugh, but it hurt and then she asked, "What about Daddy's mine?"

"I don't think Daddy's going to work his mine anymore. He's working for the Defender Mine."

Hibbard was right. Daddy walked away from the Ferguson Mine just like he had walked away from the farm in Fontana. He insisted that if he had more capital he could have gotten at the rich vein of gold. But he needed better tools, more powerful machines, and that required more money. There was no more money. Mother was tired of waiting for the Ferguson Mine to start providing for the family. And she flatly refused "to throw more money down that hole." She was tired of the promises just out of reach. Now Daddy had a job at the Defender Mine, a big operation up the

Defender Grade. He would bring home a paycheck. Not much, but more than he ever got out of the Ferguson Mine.

Acorns

"Grandpa! Brubby! Over here! I found a bunch of them."

Marian's head popped out from between two bushes and then disappeared again. Billy, the goat, leapt over the bushes toward Marian's laughter. Hibbard ran over and dove under a branch, disappearing. Grandpa took out his pocket watch and checked the time as Mother shushed the children. Daddy was inside sleeping and would have to get up at dinner time to go up the long windy road to the Defender Mine.

Mother looked around frantically, "Where has that girl gotten off to? I heard her just a minute ago. Marian?"

"She's just past those bushes," Grandpa reassured her.

"The doctor said she still has to be careful."

"Don't worry, Helen. Hibbard's with her."

"I just wish she wouldn't go running off."

"You don't want them staying here while Big Hib's trying to sleep."

"But Dad, I just get so scared. I couldn't protect Betty Jane. When Marian got so sick, I just knew I was going to lose her too. I couldn't live through that again."

"I'm sorry we weren't here to help you."

"You had to be in Oakland with Mildred; that's where your doctors are. Besides we didn't know what we were getting ourselves into up in these mountains."

"I just wish I could have timed my heart attack better." Grandpa gave Mother a stiff hug and looked around, "And now, where has Marian got off to?"

"Thanks, Dad. There are so many dangers up here, and I can't watch her every minute."

"Don't worry, Helen, I'll keep an eye on her."

As Grandpa ducked behind the bush with his canvas tarp, Marian knelt with the skirt of her dress held like a hammock. She crawled along picking up acorns and dropping them in the skirt of her dress. Hibbard bobbed up and down plucking up each acorn and tossing them into Marian's skirt hammock.

"Brubby, LOOK," Marian squealed. "I found an arrowhead!"

"Let me see."

"See."

"Nah, that's just a rock."

"Ahhhhh! Are you sure? Maybe the tip just broke off."

"Nah, it's just a rock."

"Ahh! I thought for sure it was an arrowhead this time."

"We gotta ask Lily where to find some."

"Maybe over by the grinding rocks. Grandpa, can we go across to the old grinding rocks?"

"There's lots of acorns here, let's get the rest of these first," said Grandpa.

After Marian filled her skirt with acorns, she dumped them onto the tarp that Grandpa dragged along. Sometimes it looked as if Grandpa was thinking of something else. Grandpa had made a fortune in Ohio. That was before the crash. And now he dragged a canvas tarp around behind his grandchildren as they collected thousands of acorns to sell to a hog farmer for a few pennies. Times had changed. How could he have had so much and now so little? Marian and Hibbard ran around collecting more acorns.

"Grandpa, a girl at school said that acorns make the pork bitter," said Marian.

"The pigs have to eat. I'm sure if the farmer had something better to feed them, he would."

"Come on, Sis," said Hibbard, "I counted, and we have twenty-eight cents so far. If we find a lot today and tomorrow, then we could give Mother thirty-five cents."

"Would that be enough for a bag of groceries?" Marian asked.

"Almost."

They spent the afternoon collecting acorns, inching their way through the woods until they got to the old Indian grinding rocks. Not much acorn collecting happened there because the children were far more interested in trying to find arrowheads, and Grandpa was watching out for rattlesnakes. They headed back before nightfall. Grandpa dumped the acorns on the huge pile in front of the cabin. Hibbard got two buckets to fill with water at the well for evening dishes. Mother stuck her head out the door wiping her hands on a dish towel, waved at Grandpa and Marian, and then disappeared back into the kitchen. Grandpa checked the time on his pocket watch. Then Marian and Grandpa filled three large gunny sacks with acorns.

After dinner, the hog farmer came by, tossed the gunny sacks into the back of his truck and counted out three pennies into Hibbard's hands and three into Marian's. The two smiled at each other as they did the math in their heads. They ran back into the house and poured all thirty four pennies onto the table and announced, "You can buy whatever you want!"

Mother clapped her hands with surprise and smiled at Grandpa. Then she hugged the children and said, "We'll have an extra bag of groceries this month."

Each month the family went on a day trip to Jackson to get all the supplies for that month. But if they needed something between their trips, they were able to buy from the delivery truck. The Graven Engel truck came up from Stockton and delivered groceries to small stores in the communities of the foothills. As it came up Highway 26, it stopped and honked from the road. Mother occasionally walked down to buy a little something like yeast to bake bread, or margarine, or sugar.

A few days after the children gave their mother the acorn money, Mother called Marian and Hibbard to walk her down to the truck. She held five of the pennies from the hog farmer. She asked the driver for bread. The children looked at each other questioning. The driver rummaged in the back and presented a bag to Mother. The store had baked it, sliced it, packaged it. Marian and Hibbard's eyes widened. Store-bought bread? What a surprise! They opened the bag right there. The inside of the bread was white instead of brown. It was so light and fluffy. It was airy. Hibbard took a slice in his hand and squeezed it into a ball. The children giggled and ate one slice after another. When they showed Daddy, he took the remaining loaf in this hands and flipped through the slices like a deck of cards and said, "What is this world coming to when a woman can't slice her own bread?"

Tea in Apricot Orchard

When Aunt Mildred heard that Grandpa helped with gathering acorns, she couldn't believe it. Mother and Grandma tried to explain that Grandpa wanted to gather acorns with the children because it made him feel like he was contributing to the family. Grandma and Grandpa had come to Glencoe to help Mother care for Marian after her appendectomy, but Grandpa also needed care because he had a heart attack after leaving Fontana. These days he moved slowly and got out of breath quickly. Aunt Mildred insisted that Grandpa needed to be protected from the rough and harsh living in Glencoe. She wanted him to come back to Oakland and live with her, but Grandpa put off leaving until the end of the school year when Marian's family prepared to leave Glencoe. Daddy had heard about a job in Willows that provided housing for families.

When the time came, Daddy packed Grandma and Grandpa's things in the truck and drove them to Aunt Mildred's in Oakland. Then he came back to pack the family's things before heading to Willows. When they arrived at an apricot orchard, they saw tents pitched around the perimeter. Mother simply sighed as they found a spot to pitch their tent and set up their living quarters.

"It's just going to be for one harvest," said Daddy, "and then we'll be in Placerville. We'll have a beautiful home. I've got the job at the mine, but it's going to take a little more time."

"Uh huh," said Mother.

Daddy and Hibbard got hired to pick the apricots, and Mother and Marian to cut them for drying. It was not so different from what Marian remembered in Fontana. But now they had a tent instead of a chicken coop and other workers' tents surrounded them. It was just as blistering hot as in Fontana, maybe even hotter.

On the walk from their tent to work, Marian heard different languages spoken. Each family lived out their lives in front of the others with only a piece of canvas to separate one family from another. Marian remembered the little angel in the neighboring tent from West Point and looked around hoping to find her again. Whole families worked in the orchard together, four-years-olds to people older than Grandpa. Like the other children, Marian and Hibbard were expected to work. Each day, they started with the rising sun and ended when it set. Only babies and toddlers

didn't work. The babies were cared for by older siblings or swaddled on their mother's back, and toddlers were within sight of their mother, if not within her reach.

Mother hated the layer of dirt on everyone and everything. Even the water was dirty, so Mother boiled and strained it. She insisted Marian and Hibbard wear clean clothes to the orchard each day. At night, they read poetry to each other.

"I liked listening to your Mama read last night. How long have you been a 'fruit tramp'?"* asked a neighbor girl.

"Fruit tramp?"

"That's what they call us. Don't you follow the crops?"

"No. We're just here for this harvest."

"I thought you might be kinda' new."

"How long have you been working in the fields?"

"A couple of seasons, since we lost our farm in Oklahoma 'cuz of the dust storms."*

"Dust storms?"

"It was so bad Mama used to tie a rope around my waist when I went out to milk the cow."

"Why?"

"So I wouldn't get lost."

"How could you get lost going from the house to the barn?"

"When I got to the barn, I couldn't see the house through all the swirling dirt. All day long we'd try to keep our things clean but it was impossible. Near went crazy trying, though. The sky would go dark in the middle of the day, dark enough you'd think it was night. Here the sky is blue and no dirt to speak of."

"Sounds scary."

"Nah, not really. You get used to it. I love it out here, though. Everything's green. Back home nothin' grew. All browns and greys, just dirt as far as you could see. Nothin' can live in that. But here the plants grow and there are apricots to harvest. Everything grows here."

Marian's family worked hard each day — ten hours, sometimes more. No one complained. Everyone worked hard. They worked when they didn't feel like it, when they were tired, when they were sweltering. They worked as long as there was work to be done.

One day Marian and her Mother were walking back to their tent from the field. Marian wiped the back of her neck and felt the grime left there by the combination of sweat and dirt. She wiped her hands on her dress. They passed a tent where a Mexican family lived. The mother and teenage daughters were busy patting their hands together flattening dough into tortillas and plopping them on a griddle. They cooked one side and then picked them up with their fingers and turned them over to cook the other side. Then they patted a new tortilla. The quickness of their hands mesmerized Marian. The mother smiled and motioned Marian to come over. Marian and her mother walked over and smiled, nodding. The mother only spoke Spanish, and the daughter translated, "My mother wants to give your girl a tortilla with sugar."

"Oh, gracias," said Mother remembering the Spanish she knew in Puerto Rico.

Marian was already taking a bite. And smiling, saying, "Delicious. Hmm."

"Deliciosa," said the teenager laughing.

"Si," said the mother, sharing the laugh.

The next day Marian's mother stopped by after work and brought the family a jar of orange marmalade. The mother invited her to sit and have some tea. They each sat on a wooden crate and sipped tea from china teacups. Marian thought it strange that this family had china in the orchard. The woman's had a little chip on the rim of the cup, but Mother's cup had no chip.

The woman said something to her daughter, who went into the tent and returned with a book. The woman set her teacup down on the crate between them and opened the book up and read in Spanish, a poem. Marian couldn't understand the words, but she could hear the rhythm and the sounds that the words made, and there was a beauty. The daughter took a bandana and dunked it in cool water and wrapped it around Marian's neck. A shiver of coolness warded off the sweltering heat as they sipped and listened.

On the way back to their tent, Mother said, "I never would have guessed it — tea and poetry in an orchard. You never know. You just never know."

For the rest of the harvest, the women and children took turns visiting one another. Sometimes the woman and her daughters came to Marian's tent and sometimes Marian and her mother went to theirs. They shared tea and poetry. They loved reading and listening to each other. During these visits, Marian noticed that both mothers had a certain look on their face — as if they were each remembering a different time and place.

Placerville

Marian's family left the apricot orchard with high hopes. Daddy was going to work at the Empire Mine. They needed a mine supervisor and were very impressed with Daddy's credentials. The family moved back to the mountains proud that Daddy was hired at such a big operation. In Placerville, Mother would have a proper house with a lawn and a garden, right across the street from the school.

As they walked through the house, Marian gasped, realizing she would have her very own bedroom. And the outhouse was indoors, a little bathroom between the bedrooms. No more going outside to the outhouse in the middle of the night! Marian and Hibbard ran through the house exploring. Then the family unpacked and moved their belongings in. When they were all moved in, Hibbard and Marian went outside to explore. They had never had a lawn. They lay on it and gazed up at the clouds floating over the blue sky. It was so peaceful.

Marian turned to Hibbard and said, "School starts next week. What if I don't make any friends?"

But Hibbard said, "Golly Ned, we should be good at it by now, four schools in four years."

"Yeah, I guess you're right."

On the first day of school Ronarda Cook befriended Marian. Ronarda had a lot of girlfriends, and so Marian instantly had friends. Ronarda played violin, too, and they started playing duets together. Everything was working out.

Everything was working out, until the day Daddy came home from work drunk. Daddy had never been drunk before. He stumbled into the house, doors slamming and voice yelling. Mother immediately scurried around the house shutting all the windows. Marian had seen men drunk before up in West Point and she even heard about it in Fontana but never her Daddy. Hibbard and Marian peered downstairs at Mother and Daddy. That's when they heard that Daddy didn't *have* the job, that he *almost* had the job. He just needed to pass the physical. But the doctor found he had silicosis, the "miners' lung disease." Mother heard Daddy say he didn't have the job and nothing else.

"You moved us here for a 'maybe'? For another one of your 'dreams'?"

Daddy pushed Mother away, and she tripped

over the rug. The children ran downstairs, and Hibbard knelt over Mother. Daddy took a step toward them, but Marian stood in front of Mother staring at him.

"Daddy, what's happened to you?" she asked.

"I found out I'm dying that's what happened. And your Mother doesn't care."

"Oh Daddy, don't say that."

"Don't you sass me," Daddy said swatting at Marian.

"Pop!" yelled Hibbard.

"My whole family has turned against me," Daddy said. "My whole family!"

He stumbled out the door and fell down the front steps. Hibbard ran after Daddy, caught up with him, but Daddy shook himself free and walked away from the house.

"Pop! Come back, Pop!"

Mother came to the doorway, looked around at the neighboring houses and in hushed tones said, "Hibbard don't yell. The neighbors will hear. Come on, back inside."

That night after Marian and Hibbard were in bed, they heard the mumbling of their parents' voices. In the morning, Daddy packed his things in his old canvas duffel bag. He looked terrible. If he had looked up, he would have seen Marian at the top of the stairs. He didn't say anything as he shut the front door. Mother was in the kitchen fixing oatmeal, and Marian could see she had been crying.

"Daddy's going prospecting in the mountains."

"When's he coming back?"

"Don't know."

"Where are we going to live?"

"Right here."

"How can we pay rent?"

"Daddy gave me some money for a few months."

Marian could see that the questions were upsetting Mother, so she just said, "Oh."

None of the neighbors knew what had happened or if they did, they didn't say anything. Daddy was around very seldom that year, and Marian never knew when he was going to show up. She would find him in the morning sleeping in his clothes on the couch. He stayed for one or two days and then he left. Mother said he was chasing his dream, placer mining in the Trinity Alps.

The town of Placerville was built in a canyon. Ronarda Cook lived on one side of the canyon and Marian lived on the other. At night from their bedroom windows they would talk to each other using flashlights and Morse code.* Both of their fathers had been in the Great War, and the girls had learned the code from them years ago. So Marian might ask,

".-- .... .- -   .- .-. .   -.-- --- ..-
.-- . .- .-. .. -. --.   - --- -- --- .-.
.-. --- .--"

And Ronarda might answer,

"-- -.--   .--. ..- .-. .--. .-.. .
-.. .-. .   ..."

In March, Marian invited Ronarda over to spend the night for her birthday. Marian had never had a sleepover and only once before had a friend come over for her birthday. It was years ago in Fontana, Doris Ingold came over, and Mother wouldn't let Doris go into the house. She set up a birthday table outside under the eucalyptus trees. But this birthday they had a house that Mother was not ashamed of, a bedroom all of Marian's own and a friend with whom she giggled and shared secrets. When Mother knocked on the door announcing that a package had arrived, they were up in Marian's room. It was from Aunt Mildred. The girls ran downstairs; Marian carefully opened the wrapping paper so Mother could iron it to be saved for another present. When she opened the box, they squealed. It was a Deanna Durbin* dress.

"Try it on, try it on," said Ronarda clapping her hands.

Marian put it on in the bathroom and swirled out, striking a Deanna Durbin pose. Ronarda applauded and insisted that Marian wear the dress to school. Marian floated down the front steps of the school in that dress.

The next night they met at their separate bedroom windows after dinner and dotted and dashed their way through a conversation. Mother called up to Marian and Hibbard; it was time to do their chore. So Marian said,

"... . .   -.-- --- ..-   .- -   ... -.-. .... --- --- .-.."

"--. --- --- -..   -. .. --. .... - " said Ronarda.

Marian did not want to tell Ronarda what her chore was and she hoped no one saw. She and Hibbard went outside with two pairs of scissors. They walked down the stone steps and onto the lawn. They each knelt down and began trimming the grass with their scissors. Embarrassed that they didn't own a lawn mower, Mother didn't want anyone to find out. Mother could hide how they were just scraping by, how very poor they were, but she felt a shaggy lawn would broadcast their poverty. So a couple nights a week Marian and

Hibbard crawled around on the lawn trimming the grass and ducking headlights when cars went by.

One weekend, Aunt Mildred came to take Mother to San Jose. Mother knew the only way Marian and Hibbard would be able to go to college was if they lived in a college town, so they could live at home while they went to college. Aunt Mildred told Mother she could take in boarders who were college students and needed a place to live. Mother fell in love with San Jose, a beautiful small college town. The tree-lined streets were quiet and there were many lush gardens. They would wait until the end of the school year when Marian graduated eighth grade.

The next time Daddy came home, Mother announced her plan. Daddy liked the idea but suggested they live in Chico instead so that Daddy could continue prospecting in the Trinity Alps.

"No," said Mother flatly. "The children and I are moving to San Jose. You can come or not."

On moving day, Daddy was there. He and Hibbard packed the truck while Marian picked wild sweet-pea flowers. Hibbard said goodbye to his friends, and Mother went through the house one more time to make sure she hadn't left anything behind. All four of them piled into the truck, and as Daddy pulled out Marian tossed her sweet-pea bouquet to her dear friend, Ronarda Cook. The sweet goodbye to Ronarda also signaled the family's goodbye to the mountains and — as time would show — to the Great Depression.

Epilogue

Marian's family moved to San Jose with the money Aunt Mildred gave them. They rented a seven-bedroom house at 86 South 12th, a tree-lined street just blocks away from San Jose State. Mother opened her new home to boarders, advertising in the college housing office and the music department. In the corner room upstairs, a drummer by the name of Wally Trabing practiced a couple hours each afternoon to the annoyance of neighbors. Dr. Robinson, a philosophy professor at the college, lived with his father, Mr. Robinson, who taught Marian how to play pinochle, which they played most days after school. Lloyd Holt was a boarder who played sax and kept Marian's family and the other boarders laughing with his joking nature. His roommate, Tubby, played the classical trombone and went out of his way to be kind to Marian, walking her to school and carrying her violin. A clarinet player lived downstairs in a small alcove off the kitchen. In exchange for room and board, he swept and washed the floors and dusted the furniture. Tommy Finnerty, who worked for a paper company as a salesman, lived with Marian's family until he married. Having the house full of boarders was lively but also a lot of work: cooking, cleaning, washing, laundry, ironing, and dishes. At night, when Marian and Hibbard stood at the sink — washing, rinsing, and drying — they sang duets and danced.

Moving to San Jose meant another new school, the fifth in five years. Marian felt out of place when she walked into the high school. Having lived in the country all her life, she went to school with a clean face and knee high stockings, but girls her age in San Jose wore makeup and nylons and looked like women. Once again she felt like an outsider. For a lonesome month, she floundered without any friends. Then Betty Ann invited Marian to the movies, and that began a friendship that spanned seven decades.

The streets of San Jose were different from what Marian was used to. She had sidewalks for the first time. At Christmas time, Aunt Mildred gave Marian and Hibbard roller skates. They remembered reading "Hans Brinker or the Silver Skates" years before and were delighted to put on skates for the first time. A neighborhood girl, June, taught Marian how to skate. She was an expert who could walk up the front steps in her skates and roll right into Marian's house. The first time she did so, Marian laughed and Mother chased her out in utter shock. While many young people went to roller rinks to skate, Hibbard and Marian became fabulous skaters on the streets. Throughout high school, they spent many hours zipping up and down the sidewalk, without a care in the world.

For the entire year before moving to San Jose, Daddy had been unemployed. After getting diagnosed with silicosis, he knew his days of going down in the gold mines were over. He left Marian, her mother, and brother in Placerville to try prospecting in the streams of the Trinity Mountains. He found just enough to keep him going back. However, once they arrived in San Jose, he began searching for regular employment and found a carpentry job at Fort Ord in Monterey. Because of the distance between Monterey and San Jose, he stayed in Monterey during the week and only came home on weekends. War was eminent and the Army needed barracks. The sawdust wasn't good for his lungs, but it was steady work until World War II ended. By that time, Daddy had saved enough to buy a prune orchard and then an even bigger apricot orchard. Daddy lived another twenty years. He often coughed and was short of breath, but he continued working hard, tending the orchard and raising chickens until the end. When he had a free day, he'd head into the mountains to study rock formations and prospect for gold, having never given up on his dream of one day striking it rich.

On the weekends after chores and homework were done, the household often gathered to sing around the piano that had traveled with them all those miles like a member of the family. Mother played this old friend. Marian played the violin, and the boarders chimed in on the sax, clarinet, drum, and trombone. Daddy and Hibbard added their voices, singing in harmony. They sang hymns, "La Golondrina," classical tunes, songs from Mother and Daddy's courting days, like "There's a long, long trail a-winding into the land of our dreams." Sometimes they even sang contemporary songs like "Side by Side,"*

Oh, we ain't got a barrel of money
Maybe we're ragged and funny
But we'll travel along
Singin' a song, side by side.

The music seemed to tell the story.

Appendix

Note to the Reader

p.2 Great Depression – a devastating time in America's history when the country's economic structures crumbled, people lost their savings, their houses, their jobs. Lasting about a decade, it had its start on October 29, 1929, Black Tuesday, with the stock market crash. One fourth of American adults lost their jobs. The average person barely scraped by. Many children went hungry and had no shoes or warm clothes. You might want to read: <u>Children of the Great Depression</u> by Russell Freeman or <u>Dear Mrs. Roosevelt: Letters from Children of the Great Depression</u> edited by Robert Cohen.

p.2 Oral History / Family Stories –

I am delighted that you want to know more about interviewing elders. It is a very special encounter when young and old come together to develop a deeper understanding. It is an opportunity to listen and to share, a gift given in both directions. Below are some tips to get you started:

First ask yourself, do I want to conduct an oral history interview or do I want to record family stories? Oral history means you will be sharing and archiving the interviews with a larger audience than just your family and friends. If the person you want to interview was a participant in a historical event or movement, you may want to consider sharing the interview with an archive or library. If you want to do oral histories, I would strongly recommend either <u>Recording Oral History</u> by Valerie Yow or <u>Doing Oral History</u> by Donald Ritchie.

However, for most of you, it is just a matter of scheduling the time to sit down to listen to your family member's stories. Whether you are recording oral histories or family stories, it helps to be prepared. Here are my steps:

1. Select the person you will interview.
2. Select what time period or event you want for the focus of the interview.
3. Research the period or event. You will need to know as much as possible about the time period or event so you can create a list of questions and topics.
4. Make a list of questions/topics. There are two kinds of questions:
   a. Open-ended questions encourage the interviewee to tell a story.
   b. Closed-ended questions are

answered with yes/no or a few words. (When you are coming up with your questions you are welcome to contact me, or you can review some at www.storycorps.org or in the book <u>Legacy</u> by Linda Spence.)

5. Prepare three open-ended questions to every closed-ended question.
6. Equipment: Get your recording equipment ready before the interview.
    a. Practice using the equipment to be sure you know how all the functions work.
    b. Technology is changing quickly. Use the best equipment available; a digital recorder is preferable.
    c. Put fresh batteries in your recorder and bring an extra set of batteries.
    d. Bring external plug-in and extension cord.
    e. If you are using a digital recorder, bring an extra memory/SD card.
    f. Do a sound check to test the

sound quality; make any needed adjustments.
7. Environment: Select a quiet room, free of noise or distractions for your interview.
   a. Avoid TV, radio, motors running, fans, dishwasher, dogs barking, phone ringing, and people coming and going.
   b. Put the recorder between you and the interviewee, maybe on a small portable table. Do a sound check to ensure the placement of the microphone is correct.
   c. Have a glass of water (without ice) for each of you. Your mouth may get dry, but you don't want the recorder to pick up the sound of the clinking of the ice.
8. At the beginning of each interview, record an "Intro tag" with both of your names, date, location, and topic.
9. After Interview:
   a. Make two copies of the interview labeled with the intro tag information and give one to your interviewee and keep the other one

in a safe place different from the
recorder.
  b. Write interviewee a thank you note.

It Began with a Crash

p.12 Fontana Farms was a company that
sold five- to ten-acre plots of land to families and
retirees wanting to move from Los Angeles to the
country. A. B. Miller founded the town and owned
Fontana Farms Company and the Fontana Land
Company. He had an elaborate plan called
"partnership of hens and oranges. " The plan gave
farmers an income from selling eggs and chickens
until the citrus could support them. The chicken
manure provided fertilizer for the orange groves.
The plan appealed to buyers with limited money
who dreamed of country living and farm ownership.
Buyers could put a little money down and pay the
balance in installments semiannually.

  p.14 Mother's Lemon Meringue Pie Recipe

Recipe for pie crust:
1 $\frac{1}{2}$ cups all-purpose flour
Pinch of salt
$\frac{1}{2}$ cup lard
3-4 T. cold water

In a bowl, combine flour and salt. Cut in lard until it crumbles. Sprinkle in water, a tablespoon at a time, until pastry holds together. Shape into ball; chill for 30 minutes. On a lightly floured board, roll out dough to 1/8 inch thickness. Flute edges and bake until golden.

Recipe for pie filling:
1 cup sugar
1 ¼ cups water
1 T. butter
¼ cup cornstarch
3 T. cold water
6 T. lemon juice
1 tsp. grated lemon peel
3 egg yolks
2 T. milk

Combine sugar, water, and butter; heat until sugar dissolves. Add cornstarch blended with cold water; cook slowly until clear, about 8 minutes. Add lemon juice and peel; cook 2 minutes. Slowly add egg yolks beaten with milk; bring to boil. Cool. Pour into cooled baked shell.

Recipe for Meringue:
3 egg whites
6 T. sugar
1 tsp. lemon juice

Beat egg whites stiff but not dry; add sugar gradually; add lemon juice at the last. Spread over cooled filling, sealing to edges of pastry. Brown in moderate oven (350 degree) 13-15 minutes.

p.15 Stock Market – is a way that individuals can invest in a company. Ownership in the company is divided up into small units/stocks/shares. People can buy a "share." Then the company uses that money to grow or buy materials needed to make their product. When the company makes money, the investors or shareholders also make money because their shares are worth more. When the company loses money, the shares are worth less. Ideally, investors buy shares at a low price and then sell them at a high price. During the crash in 1929, shares that had been bought at a high price could only be sold for very low prices, so investors lost the money they had invested.

p.17 Bear Market is when the price of stocks decline over a period of more than two months. Investors become pessimistic or worried that they will lose their money.

p.17 Bull Market is when the price of stocks rise. Investors become optimistic or hopeful that they will make money.

A New Friend

p.23 Santa Ana winds are very strong winds in Southern California that can exceed 40 miles an hour. They occur during the autumn or winter. Most people who grew up in Southern California have a story about the Santa Ana winds. One day, when I was in Fontana doing research for this book, I had to fight the wind to get into the Fontana Historical Society building. It reminded me of the tornado in the "Wizard of Oz." I thought the little building was going to be lifted right off its foundation.

p.23 Migration during the Depression – Millions of people were homeless and moved around the country in search of work. Sometimes whole families traveled together and other times the families stayed behind or moved in with relatives while the father went job hunting. Children as young as twelve left home to forage for themselves and search for work. People slept on the side of the road (like in this story), in abandoned barns, houses, or railcars and in small communities called "Hoovervilles" where shacks were made out of cardboard, scraps of tin or wood, and other discarded materials.

p.24 Anty Over was a popular childhood game. There are two teams, one on each side of a shed or table. One of the teams has a ball and is "It." During the Depression if the children did not have a ball, they made one out of cloth rolled up and tied with string. Marian remembers using a rock, but it is a lot safer and more fun to use a ball or even a stuffed animal. The team that is "It" yells "anty over" and throws the ball to someone on the opposing team. If the ball is dropped, then their team is "It." If they catch the ball, then both teams quickly change sides while the person who caught the ball tries to hit someone from the other side with the ball or catch/tag them. If they succeed, that person comes to their side. The game ends when one team is eliminated or the school bell rings.

p.27 **Great War** – another name for World War I.

p.27 **Rouge Bouquet bombardment** was an event during World War I that occurred in France on March 7, 1918. There were 21 casualties, all from one platoon. Joyce Kilmer wrote a poem, "Rouge Bouquet," to commemorate the soldiers from his unit who died.

p.29 **Veterans Bonus** was a compensation for veterans that reflected the difference between what they were paid as soldiers and what they would have made if they were not enlisted.

For domestic service, the bonus was a dollar for every day of service up to $500 and for overseas service it was $1.25 for up to $625. After the Great War, WWI, the soldiers were given certificates and told that they would not receive cash payments for their bonus until 1944. The veterans waited, but when the Depression hit, they argued that they could wait no longer. They needed what was rightfully theirs. Marian's family got their bonus while they were living in the mountains right before Marian had appendicitis.

p.29 Sergeant Walter Waters was the leader of the Bonus Army. In 1932 during the spring and summer, 43,000 people gathered with the Bonus Army in support of the cash payments for the veterans bonus certificates. Thousands of veterans' families camped on the lawn of the Capitol, but on July 28, 1932, the veterans were dispersed by force under the leadership of Douglas MacArthur and George Patton by order of President Hoover. Four demonstrators were killed and over 1000 demonstrators were injured as well as 69 police and military.

p.29 Boulder/Hoover Dam – Building the dam was one of the largest projects during the Great Depression, employing thousands of people. It was built on the border of Nevada and Arizona to control floods and provide irrigation water and hydropower from the Colorado River. The dam was conceived in the 1920s, but construction didn't start until 1931. The dam was completed in 1936. Originally called the Boulder Dam, it was renamed Hoover Dam upon completion.

Eucalyptus Playground

p.33 Basque Sheepherders – Basque people are an ethnic group who came to America from a region in Europe that straddles the borders of Spain and France. A couple times a year, Basque sheepherders led their sheep from the San Bernadino Mountains to Los Angeles to be sold. They stopped in open fields to spend nights, coming and going without notice. They communicated with each other by carving pictures or words in thousands of aspen trees along their route. Their carvings are called arborglyphs.

Trains, Cookies, and Tinsel

p.39 Patsyette Doll – The Patsyette doll was in the Patsy Ann family of dolls. Patsy Ann was released in June 1929, months before the stock market crash. These dolls were made out of composite material. They sold for five dollars and were very popular during the 1930s.

p.44 Jam Cookie Recipe

5 ½ T. butter or lard
1 cup sugar
1 egg
¼ cup milk
2 tsp. baking powder
½ tsp. salt
2 cups flour
1 tsp. vanilla

Cream butter; add sugar, well beaten egg and milk; add sifted and mixed dry ingredients; add vanilla. Toss on floured board and roll out. Cut out with a circular cookie cutter. Half of the circles will be the bottom of the cookie and the other half will be the cover. Place spoonful of jelly in the center of the bottom circles. Use a thimble to cut a hole in the center of the cover circles. Place cover on top of jelly bottom ones, pinch edges to keep the two layers together. Bake in moderate oven until done.

.

Shaking Earth

p.49 Long Beach Earthquake, March 10, 1933, 5:55pm – magnitude of 6.4. One hundred-twenty people died and the quake caused millions of dollars in property damage. Field's Act was passed one month later on April 10, 1933. Many school buildings were damaged and 230 became unusable. If the earthquake had hit a couple hours earlier when school was in session, the death toll would have been significantly higher. The Field's Act mandated that school buildings must be built to be earthquake resistant.

     p.53 Puerto Rico Earthquake, October 11, 1918, 10:14 a.m – magnitude of 7.5. A tsunami (tidal wave) followed the earthquake with the sea level rising five feet in Mayaguez, where Marian's mother was living and teaching. In other parts of Puerto Rico, the sea level rose over twelve feet. One hundred-sixteen people died (40 of those causalities of the tsunami), and the quake caused four million dollars in property damage.

Moving In

     p.62 "La Golondrina" – a Mexican song written by Narciso Serradell in 1862 about swallows flying far from home. If you would like to hear the song you can find versions online at youtube.

     p.65 "ya no puedo a mi masion volver" – "no more to my home can I return"

     p.65 "Ave querida, amada peregrina, Mi corazón al tuyo estrecharé" – "Cherished bird, beloved pilgrim, I will bring my heart close to yours."

Hog Ranch

p.67 Fontana Hog Ranch was part of the Fontana Farms Company. At one time, it was the largest hog ranch in the world, housing 60,000 hogs. Each day, hundreds of tons of garbage were shipped by railcar from Los Angeles to Fontana to feed the hogs. Those willing to look found silverware and other treasures accidentally tossed into the garbage. Citrus farmers used the hog manure to fertilize their trees. Fattened hogs were shipped back to Los Angeles to be slaughtered.

p.68 Daddy's poetry – Here is an example of a poem he wrote called "Business is Good":

A busy age, yes indeed!
Steam and motors, - speed! more speed!
Nations competing; fraud and cheating;
A world in a frenzy, - "wealth," its creed.

Stock markets a-flutter, gambling on
    butter;
Gambling on beans and bread;
There's a street named "Wall,"
Where the winner takes all,
Or loses his all, instead.

A chess game it is, - only faster;
With the Bulls or the Bears winning fame;
Where a "check-mate" means disaster,
And the public are pawns in the game.

The dollars aren't idle, no sir!
'Elusive' seems a far better word;
The ideal, is to catch them, my dear;
That they're idle, is rather absurd.

"Alack! Alas!" the pessimist sighs;
"The world is going to ruin!" another cries;
But the signs of the times should be
    well understood,
And in heavy type reads:
"BUSINESS IS GOOD."

Secret Hideaway
p.89 Recipe for twisters

$\frac{1}{4}$ cup butter

1 cup granulated sugar

2 well beaten eggs

4 cups sifted flour

3 tsp. baking powder

$\frac{1}{4}$ tsp. nutmeg

$\frac{1}{2}$ tsp. salt

1 cup milk

Fat for deep frying

Confectioners' sugar

Cream butter and sugar; add eggs. Sift flour with baking powder, nutmeg and salt. Add alternating with milk. Chill dough. Roll out $\frac{1}{4}$ inch thick. Cut dough into strips 1 x 8 inches. Fold each strip in half lengthwise; twist several times and pinch ends together. Deep fry and flip over in hot fat until brown. Drain on absorbent paper and cool. Sprinkle with confectioners' sugar or drizzle on watermelon syrup.

p.89 Recipe for watermelon syrup
You will need several ripe watermelons. Peel the green skin off the watermelon; then cut the whole watermelon into one-inch cubes, saving any liquid. Separate the seeds. Put the cleaned chunks through a grinder or blender, and pour through a strainer into a pot. Boil down to thick syrup. As juice boils, froth will bubble up; skim that off the top. Stir occasionally.

Moving North
   p.103 Canning – is a way of preserving cooked food by sealing it in jars.

   p.107 Auto court – These predated motels.

   p.113 Chicken feed-sack dresses – At the height of the Depression, chicken feed-sack dresses were a common sight. For most people, buying fabric for growing children's clothing was too expensive. The feed companies began to package their chicken feed in pretty flowered fabric sacks, and mothers would take their daughters to the feed stores to choose the sacks they wanted to be made into dresses. Marian didn't have dresses made from feed sacks because her mother had the trunk of old clothes she used for fabric, but she does remember kitchen towels and underwear sewn from flour and feed sacks.

Making a Splash

p.127 **Potassium permanganate** is a chemical compound that comes in a powder form. It was believed to be an antidote for rattlesnake bites. When Marian's family moved up to the mountains, Mother was terrified of rattlesnakes and insisted Hibbard carry a little pinch of the powder in his pocket wrapped in a cloth. When potassium permanganate dissolves in water, it turns the water purple, so when Hibbard swam in the Mokelumne River, he was encircled by purple water.

Tea in Apricot Orchard

p.194 **Fruit tramp** was a derogatory term for migrant farmworkers, i.e., people who followed the ripening crops, looking for work. To learn more about this kind of work, read Judy's Journey by Lois Lenski.

p.194 **Dust storms/Dust Bowl.** In the 1920s, a man-made disaster happened due to a lack of understanding regarding the ecology of the Great Plains. Farmers in the Midwest plowed the prairie grasses to plant wheat. The root systems of prairie grasses are deep so they can store moisture for long periods in the event of drought. In the 1930s, there was an extended drought and crops died, but the wheat did not have the deep roots of the prairie grasses to hold the topsoil in place. When the wind blew, it picked up the topsoil creating dust storms. These dust storms, also known as Black Blizzards, blew across the Midwest. During the storms, people's vision was impaired like on a foggy day. They could only see a few feet ahead. Everything had a layer of dirt on it, including the food. Wash hung to dry on the line got dirty before it got dry. To learn more about the Dust Bowl, read <u>Out of the Dust</u> by Karen Hesse.

Placerville

   p.202 Morse code is a system of communicating using a series of on-off tones, light, or clicks. People communicating in Morse code would have to have a good sense of tempo because the letters are communicated with a series of short and long tones or lights, so the length of each short or long unit has to be consistent.

   In the story, Marian talks with Ronarda across the canyon using flashlights, flicking the

light on and then off. Marian's first word is .-- ....
.- - For the first letter .-- she would have to flick
on her light short, long, long. Short is equivalent to
a count of one and long is equivalent to three. So,
she would turn on her light for the count of one
then off for a count of one, then on for a count of
three and off for a count of one, then on for a
count of three and off. Between letters in a word,
the light source is off for a count of three and
between words light is off for a count of seven.
Grab a flashlight, and have someone read the
following instructions:

.-- Turn flashlight on for one count, then off
for one count, on for one two three, off for one
count, on for one two three, (W) then off for one
two three.

.... Turn flashlight on for one count, then off
for one count, on for one, off for one, on for one,
off for one, on for one (H) then off for one two
three.

.- Turn flashlight on for one count, and off
for one count, on for one two three, (A) then off
for one two three.

- Turn flashlight on for one two three (T)
then off for one two three four five six seven.

Congratulations you have just said "what" in
Morse code.

Here are all the rest of the letters:

A •-   J •---   S •••
B -••• K -•-   T -
C -•-• L •-•• U ••-
D -••   M --   V •••-
E •   N -•   W •--
F ••-• O ---   X -••-
G --•   P •--• Y -•--
H •••• Q --•- Z --••
I ••   R •-•

p.203 Deanna Durbin was a movie star from 1930s, well known for wearing full-skirted dresses.

Epilogue

p.212 "Side by Side" was a popular song written by Harry Woods in 1927 [used by permission of Shapiro, Bernstein & Co., Inc. (ASCAP)].

Recommended Reading

Bendiner, Robert. _Just Around the Corner: A Highly Selective History of the Thirties._ New York: Harper and Row, 1967.

Brennan, Linda Crotta. _The Stock Market._ Mankato, MN: The Child's World, 2013.

Britten, Loretta and Brash, Sarah, ed. _Hard Times: The 30's._ New York: Time-Life Books, 1998.

Cohen, Robert, ed. _Dear Mrs. Roosevelt: Letters from Children of the Great Depression._ Chapel Hill, NC: University of North Carolina Press, 2002.

Congdon, Don, ed. _The Thirties: A Time to Remember._ New York: Simon & Schuster, 1962.

Dodge, Mary Mapes. _Hans Brinker or the Silver Skates._ New York: Tom Doherty Associates, Inc., 1993.

Evans, Walker. _Walker Evans._ New York: Aperture, 1979.

Freedman, Russell. _Children of the Great Depression._ New York: Clarion Books, 2005.

Garthwaite, Wymond. _Bread an' Jam._ New York: Harper & Brothers, 1928.

Gup, Ted. _A Secret Gift._ New York: Penguin Press, 2010.

Hesse, Karen. _Out of the Dust._ New York: Scholastic, Inc., 1997.

Horan, James D. _The Desperate Years: A Pictorial History of the Thirties._ New York: Bonanza Books, 1962.

Kennedy, David M. _Freedom from Fear: The American People in Depression and War 1929-1945._ New York: Oxford University Press, 1999.

Kyvig, David E. _Daily Life in the United States, 1920-1940._ Chicago: Ivan R. Dee, 2002.

Lenski, Lois. _Judy's Journey._ New York: J.B. Lippincott Company, 1947.

McCutcheon, Marc. The Writer's Guide to Everyday Life from Prohibition through World War II. Cincinnati, OH: Writer's Digest Books, 1995.

McElvaine, Robert S. The Great Depression: America, 1929-1941. New York: Times Books, 1993.

Mulvey, Deb, ed. 'We Had Everything But Money'. Greendale, WI: Reiman Publications, L.P., 1992.

Ritchie, Donald A. Doing Oral History. New York: Oxford University Press, 2003.

Rothstein, Arthur. The Depression Years. New York: Dover Publications, Inc., 1978.

Spence, Linda. Legacy. Athens, OH: Swallow Press, Ohio University Press, 1997.

Spyri, Johanna. Heidi. New York: William Morrow and company, 1996.

Stanley, Jerry. Children of the Dust Bowl: The True Story of the School at Weedpatch Camp. New York: Crown Publishers, 1992.

Terkel, Studs. <u>Hard Times: An Oral History of the Great Depression.</u> New York: Pantheon Books, 1970.

Thompson, Kathleen and Mac Austin, Hilary, editors. <u>Children of the Depression.</u> Bloomington, IN: Indiana University Press, 2001.

Watkins, T. H. <u>The Hungry Years: A Narrative History of the Great Depression in America.</u> New York: Henry Holt, 1999.

Wood, Linda P. <u>Oral History Projects in Your Classroom.</u> Carlisle, PA: Oral History Association, 2001.

Yow, Valerie Raleigh. <u>Recording Oral History: A Practical Guide for Social Scientists.</u> Thousand Oaks, CA: SAGE Publications, Inc., 1994.

Acknowledgments

First and foremost, gratitude abounds for Rick Restivo, Don Wolfe, and Dominick Restivo, who have lived with this project every bit as much as Marian and I did. Thank you for your unwavering support through it all.

Thank you to the wise women of W.O.W. who are each such talented writers. During the writing of this book, your patience, support, and guidance made it possible: Patricia Harrelson, Ann St. James, Shelley Muniz, Ellen Stewart, Suzan Still, Carol Biederman, Blanche Abrams, Gillian Herbert, and Christine Taylor.

In the midst of busy lives, thank you for finding the time to read the manuscript and provide invaluable insights: Bill Roberson, Faye Morrison, Patricia Whiting and Jo Radner.

Thank you for sharing your experiences of growing up during the Great Depression. Hearing your stories helped bring the times and settings more fully alive: Don Cuneo, Jim Porteous, Ailene Watson Haley, Lois Pool, Noema Cooper, Jo Amato, Lavonna Eddy Mechling, Rosemary Bosse Faulkner, Jerry & Venita Meyers, Ben Carlton, Lois Noble, Marcie Sowa, Elizabeth Gillespie, Benny Castelini, Eldon Kahny, Irene Rasmussen, Fred Hampel, and Constance Crawford.

While doing research, the Fontana Historical Society, and particularly Tonia Lewis and Johnnie Long, went "above and beyond." Thank you for all your help searching through historical records and publications.

Also thanks to Fontana, Tuolumne, Calaveras and UC Berkeley Bancroft libraries; Fontana Women's Club, Fontana Community Church, central records at Fontana Unified School District, Clara Keirns, Maggie Beck, and Calaveras Historical Society.

Thank you Gillian Herbert and Melody Baker for guiding the publication of this book.

A huge thank you to Patricia Harrelson and Sharon Moore, who each kept me on track and moving forward.

Thank you to my family who found their way through hard times and brought a tremendous richness to my life: Grandma Rae, Grandpa Johnny, Grandma and Grandpa Moore, Aunt Lois, Uncle Ted, Auntie Weeze, Nani, Papa and my mom, Patricia Whiting.

And finally, with the deepest gratitude, I thank Marian for sharing your memories, your lessons, and your friendship. From our first interview eight years ago, I have felt honored to know you and hear your stories. Thank you for passing them on.

About the Author

Cynthia Restivo, a professional storyteller, enjoys listening to stories as much as telling them. She teaches storytelling to the next generation at Aspire Public Schools and as a freelance artist in Northern California. She lives with her family in the Sierra Foothills near Yosemite. When trying out new stories, her husband and three children have always been her first audience.

Cynthia co-produced two award winning CDs of stories and songs, Storyquilters and Blackberry Love. This is Cynthia's first book. Visit her website at: www.cynthiarestivo.com

In addition to writing and illustrating picture books, **Linda Knoll** is an artist, graphic designer and art teacher. She coordinates education programs at CCAA's Mistlin Gallery. Having lived all her life in Central California, she strives to share the San Joaquin Valley's richness with children of all ages. Her published picture books include "Over in the Valley" and "Patient for Pumpkins." Visit her at www.lindaknollart. blogspot.com

Marian Moore Wolfe grew up in California during the Depression. She married her college sweetheart, Don Wolfe, 66 years ago and the couple has three lovely daughters: Cathleen, Patti, and Debbie. She has worked with children with disabilities, both as an Occupational Therapist and as an Aide in Special Education classrooms. She enjoys working in her garden and traveling with Don in their Volkswagon Vanagon.